studia ANALECTA BIBLICA 17

Jean-Noël Aletti

Without Typology – No Gospels

A Suffering Messiah:
A Challenge for Matthew, Mark and Luke

Pontificia Università Gregoriana
Pontificio Istituto Biblico

ROMA 2022

Cover: Serena Aureli
Typesetting by the Author

© 2022 Pontifical Biblical Institute
Gregorian & Biblical Press
Piazza della Pilotta, 4 - 00187 Roma, Italy
www.gbpress.org - info@biblicum.com

979-12 5986-**008**-8

TABLE OF CONTENTS

PART TWO
THE PROPHETIC TYPOLOGY AND LUKE'S CULTURE

FOREWORD

In the preceding essay entitled *The Birth of the Gospels as Biographies*, published by GBPress in 2017, I have presented a sizeable challenge faced by the first Christian generation, that of writing a life (in Greek, a *bios*) of Jesus, although at that time there had only been *bioi* of illustrious men. Jesus had indeed neither been a great man of politics, nor a great soldier, nor a great orator, nor a great philosopher, nor a great historian nor a great scholar. Far from being recognized and admired in his small country, the Palestine of that day, he was considered a blasphemer, a man who had seduced and misled the people. Why the first disciples had to take up the challenge and how they did so was the subject of this first essay.

The challenge was all the greater for the first disciples who announced a *Crucified Messiah* or even a *Suffering Messiah*, which for us, Christians of today, is an oxymoron but was for our Jewish brothers a contradiction, for the messianic figures, as announced in the Scriptures and in the intertestamental Jewish traditions, were all glorious. A suffering Messiah, a fortiori dying on a cross was not expected. It is, moreover, because the first disciples announced Jesus, a Messiah dying on the cross, that the Pharisee Saul had, by prosecuting them, wanted to bring to an end what he thought to be blasphemies. How those who decided to write *bioi* of Jesus were able to establish the validity of the Suffering Messiah oxymoron is the project of the present essay: they were able to meet this challenge thanks to what today is called *typology*, in other words by showing that Jesus had all the traits of biblical prophets, by his miracles but above all by the fate that was his, a fate that had been that of the prophets, about whom a then-known *topos* said that they had been rejected and that most had been put to death by their contemporaries. In short, the present essay (i) shows that without typology there would have never been gospel narratives, but it also (ii) provides some methodological reference points for New Testament exegetes, for it is not easy to determine to which figures from the Scriptures of Israel the Gospels are alluding in order to describe Jesus. If the pages that follow have as their primary readers my fellow exegetes, I only hope that they will be able to interest, indeed, raise questions for theologians who, ordinarily reflect upon typology with the help of categories that are far from those of exegetes.

My gratitude
to Peggy Manning Meyer
the translator of this essay

ABBREVIATIONS

AnBib Studia	Analecta Biblica – Studia
Bib	*Biblica*
BETL	Bibliotheca Ephemeridum Theologicarum Lovaniensium
CBQ	*Catholic Biblical Quarterly*
ETL	*Ephemerides Theologicae Lovanienses*
JBL	*Journal of Biblical Literature*
JETS	*Journal of the Evangelical Theological Society*
JSOT	*Journal for the Study of the Old Testament*
JSNT	*Journal for the Study of the New Testament*
JSNT Sup	JSNT - Supplement Series
LD	Lectio Divina
LNTS	Library of New Testament Studies
NovT Sup	Novum Testamentum – Supplements
NTS	*New Testament Studies*
RB	*Revue Biblique*
RivBib	*Rivista Biblica*
RHPR	*Revue d'Histoire et de Philosophie Religieuses*
RSR	*Recherches de Science Religieuse*
SBA	Schweizerische Beiträge zur Altertums-wissenschaft
ThLZ	*Theologische Literaturzeitung*
TOB	Traduction Œcuménique de la Bible
ThLZ	*Theologische Literaturzeitung*
TZ	*Theologische Zeitschrift*
WUNT	Wissenschaftliche Untersuchungen zum NT

PART ONE

THE SCANDAL
OF A SUFFERING MESSIAH
AND THE CRUCIAL ROLE
OF PROPHETIC TYPOLOGY IN RESPONDING

INTRODUCTION

The first part of the present essay follows upon the one on the Gospels as biographies[1], the reading of which is assumed. To this first essay, whose principal theses I dare to assume as known, I refer the reader. Nevertheless, for those who have not had the time to become acquainted with it, in several places in the chapters that follow its theses and ideas will be briefly and clearly reformulated. But as the actual subject treated here is typology, perhaps it is useful to begin by succinctly recalling what this term means and designates in general for Biblical scholars.

I. THE TYPOLOGY OF THE NEW TESTAMENT[2]

Is there a need to point out, at the start, that the term *typology* is not used by the Gospel narratives? This much later term, nevertheless, designates a reading of the Scriptures made by these narratives that one often defines thus:

> By 'typology', at least as it refers to the NT's use of the OT, is meant the perception of significant correspondences between the characteristics and circumstances of two different historical individuals,

---

[1] J.N. ALETTI, *The Birth of the Gospels as Biographies*. With Analyses of Two Challenging Pericopae (AnBib. Lectio 11), Rome 2017. Going forward, citations will be from the English translation, *The Birth of the Gospels*.

[2] Cf. N. FRYE, *The Great Code*. The Bible and Literature, Harcourt Brace, New York, 1982. As well as the collected work edited by T. KUNTZMANN, *Typologie biblique*, Cerf, coll. Lectio Divina, Paris, 2002.

institutions, or events, such that each is understood either as an antic-ipation or as a fulfillment of the other[3].

Even if the characters, events and institutions from the Old Testament are at times called prophecies in the New Testament, it seems preferable to avoid this appellation, for typology is not an oracle, a word from the Old Testament that finds its fulfillment in the New, but characters, events, etc., in other words, concrete reali-ties each having their meaning in the spatial and temporal environ-ment that was theirs[4]. This explains why, following Saint Augus-tine[5], E. Auerbach prefers to speak of 'real prophecy' (*Realpro-phetie*), from the Latin *res*[6], for "the (Old Testament) figure has as much historical reality as what it prophesizes does"[7].

The first element (Old Testament) is called the *type*, and the second, the *antitype*. This relationship justifies the overall appella-tion *typology*. The first is as well referred to as the prefiguration, and the second, who/what is prefigured, their relationship clearly indicating that typology is a "figurative interpretation"[8].

It is in this way that the New Testament places Jesus Christ in a typological relationship with several characters and realities: Isaac (because of the "Aqeda"[9]), Elijah, the Servant in Is 53 and the

---

[3] M. KNOWLES, *Jeremiah in Matthew's Gospel*. The Rejected-Prophet Motif in Matthaean Redaction, JSOT Press, coll. JSNT Sup 68, Sheffield, 1993, p. 223. One will find analogous descriptions in R. KUNTZMANN (ed.) *Typologie biblique*, pp. 267-274.

[4] On the prophecy/typology connection, see as well GROGAN, G.W., "The Rela-tionship between Prophecy and Typology", Scottish Bulletin of Evangelical The-ology 4, 1986, pp. 5-16. For the distinction between typology and allegory, one may consult R. KUNTZMANN, *Typologie biblique*, p. 270.

[5] AUGUSTINE, *City of God* 27:8.

[6] Cf. E. AUERBACH, *Figura*, Macula, Paris, [3]2017, p. 50.

[7] *Ibid.*, p. 35. For greater clarity, I have added the word in parentheses.

[8] *Ibid.*, pp. 58-72. I will henceforth consider as equivalents the expressions 'typo-logical reading' and 'figurative reading'.

[9] As Isaac was bound to the wood (Gen 22, the Hebrew verb *'aqad* means to bind), Jesus was also bound to the wood of the cross (Acts 5:30; 10:38; 13:29; Gal 3:13; 1 Pet 2:24). One has thought as well that the Aqedah was the principal source of Matthean typology.

victime of ancient sacrifices, but also Noah's ark and Baptism, the tree in Eden and the cross, the Exodus and the death/resurrection of Jesus, Elijah and John the Baptist, etc. As I have shown for Luke[10] and am proposing to show for Mark and Matthew, typological interpretation prevails in the gospel narratives. Many of the pericopae from the Synoptics were chosen because they could be used typologically, and one can for this reason say that typology has in part determined the formation of the synoptic material.

Almost always, the Christian tradition has interpreted these relationships by saying that the fulfillment assumes a superiority of the antitype over the type (Jesus is more than Jonah, more than Elijah, etc.). As one knows, the Letter to the Hebrews develops a typology in three moments: continuity, discontinuity and superiority.

We agree when it is said that the typology of the New Testament is essentially teleological, for it points out how the figures from the Old Testament have as their *telos* Christ and New Testament realities. As for Jewish typology (biblical and post-biblical), it is said to be predominantly archeologic – oriented towards an *archè* – more specifically exodic and Mosaic. It is accepted as well that New Testament typology is *salvific*, its goal being to show the salvific orientation of history.

II. A FEW IMPORTANT DISTINCTIONS

In numerous passages, the synoptic Gospels allude to the Scriptures[11]. But every allusion does not necessarily come under typology. Indeed, one will see in ch. 3, in Mk 1:2-3 the Lord (in Greek, *kyrios*) is clearly Jesus. Yet these verses of Mark are repeating Is 40:9-10 where the same word designates YHWH and thus implies that Jesus is lord like YHWH. Similarly, in Mk 7:32-37, Jesus

---

[10] ALETTI, *The Birth of the Gospels*, ch. V, pp. 89-106.

[11] See, for ex., R.B. HAYS, *Echoes of Scripture in the Gospels*, Baylor University Press, Waco, TX, 2016.

causes the mute to speak, like YHWH in Is 35:6 – the Greek term *mogilalos*[12] is found only in this verse of Isaiah and in Mk 7:32. In these two passages, Mark clearly is alluding to the Scriptures, but can one say that the relationship is typological? The definition of typology formulated by exegetes, according to which the type is inferior to the antitype, seems to be prohibited: Can YHWH, the *kyrios* of the Old Testament, be the type of Jesus and inferior to him? In short, noting scriptural echoes does not immediately mean one is dealing with typological relationships.

Another distinction to respect is the one between a typological reprise and a *synkrisis*. The latter consists in comparing characters, actions or events by indicating their points in common and their differences, the superiority of one over another, etc. The technique was widely used by the Ancients. It was part of the *progymnasmata*, exercises that young students were required to do, but it was also used by well-known writers, such as Plutarch, in his *Parallel Lives*. It is one of the favorite techniques of the evangelist Luke, who compares John the Baptist and Jesus in Lk 1–3, the shepherd and the woman in Lk 15:1-10, the two brothers in Lk 15:11-32, but who also shows, thanks to the *synkrisis*, that the apostles Peter and Paul are like Jesus[13]. But for the same reason as in the preceding paragraph, one cannot conclude that in Acts the narrator made Jesus the type of the two apostles, for he is manifestly superior to them. But if all the *synkriseis* are not typological, every typological relationship is, on the other hand, underpinned by a *synkrisis*, for it is the common traits of the type of the Old Testament and the antitype of the New that allow connecting them.

In the preceding essay, it was often a question of the necessary requisite for biographies, namely the *anagnôrisis* – the recognition of the value of a man by his contemporaries and subsequent generations[14]. For a man to be the subject of a biography (in Greek,

---

[12] The term designates deficient diction and hearing.

[13] On the generalized usage of the comparison (*synkrisis*) in the book of Acts, see Jean-Noël ALETTI, *Quand Luc raconte. Le récit comme théologie* (Lire la Bible), Paris, 1998, 69-112.

[14] ALETTI, *The Birth of the Gospels*, passim.

bios[15]), it was necessary for him to have been recognized as worthy, for there were only *bioi* of illustrious men[16]. The present essay is proposing to show that for the *anagnôrisis* of Jesus as Messiah, the gospel writers had to have recourse to typology. The typology of the Synoptics is subordinate to the *anagnôrisis*. The coming chapters will show, let us hope, that without typology, there never would have been the gospel narratives.

III. THE ESSAY'S LIMITS AND ADDRESSEES

Typology is also very present in the fourth Gospel. But here it will not be the subject of a presentation because this essay, like the preceding one, will be centered on the Synoptics, namely, the narratives of Matthew, Mark and Luke. This being said, the observations and reflections that will be proposed can, without difficulty, be applied to the Johannine narrative.

The primary addressees of this essay are New Testament exegetes, in particular specialists on the synoptic Gospels. The style, for all that, is not too abstruse, and theologians, but also those who have some biblical knowledge, will find in it, we hope, material for reflection.

---

[15] In other words, a life. The Greek substantive *biographia* is later (5th century A.D.).
[16] Cf., for ex., *De viris illustribus* by Suetonius.

CHAPTER I

THE TYPOLOGY OF THE SYNOPTICS TODAY

I. THE REASONS FOR THE TYPOLOGY OF THE SYNOPTICS

In *The Birth of the Gospels as Biographies*, I have emphasized the decisive importance of the *anagnôrisis* for the redaction of the Gospels. Because of it, the gospel writers succeeded in overcoming the handicaps that seemed to prohibit them from writing a life (a *bios*) and were able to realize their objective. For at that time there were only *bioi* of illustrious men, and it was necessary to show that Jesus was one, that he was the expected Messiah, the Son of God. Nevertheless, if by his resurrection he had become for the disciples the glorious, royal figure expected by Jewish traditions[1], the rejection of which he had been the object and his ignominious death on the cross were contrary to expectations; the Scriptures, indeed, did not announce a suffering Messiah. But, will one object, does not Jesus resurrected say in Lk 24:26-27 that, according to the Scriptures, the Christ/Messiah had to suffer? And does not Peter, following his master in this, declare in an even stronger way that "God foretold by the mouth of *all* the prophets, that his Christ should suffer" (Acts 3:18)? One, unfortunately, will not find scriptural passages announcing the sufferings of the Messiah. According to some exegetes, Is 52:13–53:12 could have been interpreted messianically

---

[1] In addition to several well-known biblical passages (Ps 2, etc.), see, for ex., 2 Baruch 30:1; 40:1-4; 70:9; 72:2; 73:1-2; Sibylline Oracles 3:49; 5:414-419; 4 Esdras 12:31-34; Psalms of Solomon 17:21-43.

by the deuterocanonical and intertestamental Jewish writings[2]. But, if it has been said that several passages from these writings are alluding to Is 52:13–53:12, for a *messianic* reprise of the figure of the Servant, on the other hand, one is left with conjectures[3]. In short, the editorial challenge faced by the first Christian generation was twofold:

- to show that Jesus merited a *bios*, that he was thus most illustrious; this difficulty was the subject of the essay mentioned above;
- to show that Jesus' sufferings and death on the cross in no way placed in question his messiahship; to do this the authors of the gospel *bioi* had to have recourse to typology. This is the subject that, touched upon in the first essay, will be treated here more fully.

The first stage of the typological approach of the synoptic narrators was to look into the Scriptures for models that allow responding to the requirement of the *bioi* of that time, namely the necessity

---

[2] Thus, M. HENGEL, "Zur Wirkungsgeschichte von Jes 53 in vosrhristlicher Zeit", in JANOWSKI B. – STUHLMACHER P. (ed.), *Der leidende Gottesknecht*. Jesaja 53 une seine Wirkungsgeschichte, Mohr Siebeck (coll. Forschungen zum Alten Testament 14), Tübingen, 1996, pp.49-91.

[3] It is hard for me to see how M. Hengel finds messianic reprises of Is 53 in the intertestamental Jewish writings. 4 Esd 7:29 recounts the oracle of God: "My son, the Messiah, will die with all those who have a human breath", which is probably repeating the idea of a messiah before reigning for a limited period, but mentions neither rejection nor suffering. For the article of J. ADNA, "Der Gottesknecht als triumierender und interzessorischer Messias. Die Rezeption von Jes 53 im Targum Jonathan", published in the same collected work as that of M. Hengel, pp. 129-158, one must not forget that the targum in question is much later than the era of the N.T. Cf. also what was said in the same years A.Y. COLLINS, "The Appropriation of Psalms of Individual Lament by Mark", in Christopher M. TUCKETT (ed.). *The Scriptures in the Gospels*, coll. BETL 131, Leuven Peeters 1997, p. 240: "Even if Psalm 22 and Isaiah 53 had not yet been interpreted messianically in the Jewish circles at the time Mark was written, it is clear that the messianic application of the individual psalms of lament found in the Gospel of Mark is well within the boundaries of acceptable Jewish exegesis…" More than a messianic application, it is a matter of a typology with the function of confronting the question of the *anagnôrisis*.

of a final and total *anagnôrisis* of Jesus. Paradoxically, the first model, faithfully followed by the Markan Passion narrative, was that of the persecuted faithful of the Psalms of supplication, a model thanks to which a horizontal or human recognition, by Jesus' coreligionists, did not or no longer had a raison d'être: like that of the persecuted innocent of the Psalms, the recognition of the being and behavior of Jesus had only to come from God alone, and that happened through the resurrection[4].

As highlighted by the tables on the common motifs of the Passion narrative of Mark and the supplications of the persecuted innocent[5], the work of the Markan narrator[6] consisted in collecting, after having noted and identified them, all the parallels common to Jesus' Passion and the supplications of the persecuted innocent. The type – the Old Testament figure – was not made in advance[7], and the operation of the *synkrisis* did not first have the goal of showing that the Old Testament motifs prefigured Jesus' sufferings and that the latter brought to their fulfillment the sufferings and cries of the innocents of the supplications: its primary role was to provide a model capable of overcoming the challenge posed by the necessity of a final *anagnôrisis*. If the recent studies on the typology of the New Testament – in particular that of the Synoptics – have especially tended towards the relationship of announcement and fulfillment that exists between the Old Testament type and the New Testament antitype[8], it is important to recall strongly that it did not constitute

---

[4] Cf. ch. 2 of *The Birth of the Gospels as Biographies,* pp. 35-38.

[5] *The Birth of the Gospels*, pp. 35-36. Also, here, pp. 50-55.

[6] It may be that the typology of the Passion narrative in Mark is anterior to the redactor's last redactional phase. This changes nothing on the reflection here undertaken on the typology of the Synoptics.

[7] My statements agree with those of Michel DENFKFN, "Jésus de Nazareth fondement atypique de la typologie chrétienne", p. 259: "There is not a type given in advance. At the beginning, there is only the antitype. All work of typology, even before claiming to illustrate, indeed to establish, a fulfillment, first begins with the affirmation of a point of view".

[8] Cf., for ex., the final overview published in R. KUNTZMANN (ed.) *Typologie biblique*, p. 269: Basically, in the typological operation "one finds the conviction

the primary objective of the redactors: the *anagnôrisis* was their primary imperative, and it remains the backdrop of their typological writing. If this change of perspective does not make all the studies published up to now meaningless, it does, nevertheless, invite the exegete to be more attentive, than up to the present has been the case, to the way in which the Synoptics elaborated their typology: where is there typology, and how to determine whether it really is a matter of typology – a term which one has too often been used and abused.

II. THE CHALLENGE OF NEW TESTAMENT TYPOLOGY

In the studies devoted to New Testament typology, it is often said that the events, circumstances, persons, peoples, institutions from the Old Testament are a preparation or a prophecy of the events, circumstances, persons, peoples and institutions of the New[9]. It is, moreover, accepted that this way of seeing the relationship between the type and the antitype actually is only describing and repeating the perspective of the writings of the New Testament, the one criticized by E. Auerbach, in his famous essay *Mimesis*[10]:

> … We find the Fathers pursuing the interpretation of reality – interpretation above all of Scripture, but also of large historical contexts, especially Roman history, for the purpose of bringing them into harmony with the Judaeo-

---

that history is being repeated and that it progresses towards a fulfillment. In the typological reprise, the old element appears as an announcement of the new element and the new as the fulfillment of the old".

[9] Several statements taken from the final overview published in KUNTZMANN (ed), *Typologie biblique*, are representative of this way of seeing; in addition to that cited in the preceding note, here is another: "[T]he meaning resides in the fulfillment of the type, which becomes a prophecy of it" (p. 273).

[10] E. AUERBACH, *Mimesis*. The Representation of Reality in Western Literature – New and Expanded Edition. Trans. Willard R. Trask, Editions Paperback 2013; (original German 1946), pp. 73-74 (at the end of the chapter on the arrest of Pierre Valvomère). On this subject, see as well Walther EICHRODT, "Is Typological Exegesis an Appropriate Method?" in C. WESTERMANN (ed.) *Essays on Old Testament Hermeneutics*, John Knox, Richmond, VA 1963, p. 225.

Christian view of history. The method employed is almost exclusively that of figures [...]. Figural interpretation "establishes a connection between two events or persons in such a way that the first signifies not only itself but also the second, while the second involves or fulfills the first. The two poles of a figure are separated in time, but both, being real events or persons, are within temporality. They are both contained in the flowing stream which is historical life, and only the comprehension, the *intellectus spiritualis*, of their interdependence is a spiritual act"[11]. In practice we almost always find an interpretation of the Old Testament, whose episodes are interpreted as figures or phenomenal prophecies of the events of the New Testament...

This type of interpretation obviously introduces an entirely new and alien element into the antique conception of history. For example, if an occurrence like the sacrifice of Isaac is interpreted as prefiguring the sacrifice of Christ, so that in the former the latter is as it were announced and promised, and the latter "fulfills" (the technical term is *figuram implere*) the former, then a connection is established between two events which are linked neither temporally nor causally – a connection which it is impossible to establish by reason in the horizontal dimension (if I may be permitted to use this term for a temporal extension). It can be established only if both occurrences are vertically linked to Divine Providence, which alone is able to devise such a plan of history and supply the key to its understanding. The horizontal, that is the temporal and causal, connection of occurrences is dissolved; the here and now is no longer a mere link in an earthly chain of events, it is simultaneously something which has always been, and which will be fulfilled in the future; and strictly, in the eyes of God, it is something eternal, something omni-temporal, something already consummated in the realm of fragmentary earthly event. This conception of history is magnificent in its homogeneity, but it was completely alien to the mentality of classical antiquity.

The historical approach cannot in fact causally connect either in time or in space the characters, events, etc., put in typological

---

[11] Auerbach is citing one of his preceding studies, "Figura", a long article published in Archivum Romanicum 22, 1938, pp. 436-489. French translation: *Figura* (Paris, Macula, ³2017). The cited passage is found on p. 65 of the French translation. English Translation: "Figura" in *Time, History, and Literature: Selected Essays of Erich Auerbach* (Princeton, Princeton University Press, 2014). One has rightly seen in this article a landmark idea of Auerbach's thought, according to which Saint Paul and the Fathers of the Church only saw, wrongly, in the Old Testament a shadow of things to come.

relationship by the gospel narratives; as only faith allows invoking the divine plan, this hermeneutic has for this reason been accused of being *deus ex machina* by so-called scientific studies. The reproach comes from most exegetes considering the type and the antitype above all as a preparation (or an announcement) and a fulfillment – the fulfillment including a surpassing of the Old Testament reality. Yet this would assume that one finds this relationship, which was only established subsequently, explicitly formulated in the Synoptics. The first question of the narrators/redactors was indeed based on facts, in other words the numerous testimonies of the crowds concerning the prophetic identity of Jesus[12]. This meant that Jesus had to give signs in order to be recognized as such. From this first acknowledgement based on his teachings and his actions, the redactors could show that Jesus had as well experienced the fate of numerous prophets, persecuted by their own people, their sufferings and persecutions being, moreover, known and diffused at the time. From works like *The Martyrdom of Isaiah*, the *Paralipomena* of Jeremiah, the *Lives of the Prophets*, written a little before our era, reflected this idea that the prophets as a whole were rejected and put to death by their contemporary Israelites, as seen in the box:

- prophets persecuted or threatened: 1 Kings 19:10, 14; 22:24, 27; 2 Kings 6:32; 2 Chron 18:23, 26; 36:16; Jer 11:21; 18:23; 38:15, 25.
- prophets put to death: Jer 26:19 (Micah); 26:20-33 (Uriah); Neh 9:26 ("they killed thy prophets"); also *The Lives of the Prophets*, a Jewish writing originally in Greek, probably from the 1st century of our era, in which it is said that Isaiah was sawn apart (1:1), Jeremiah, stoned (2:1), Ezekiel, put to death by the leader of the people (3:1), Micah, hanged (6:1), Amos, struck on his temple (7:1) and Zechariah, put to death by the king Josiah in the Temple (23:1); *The Martyrdom of Isaiah* 5:1b-10.
- the commonplace (or *topos*) is repeated in the N.T. in Mt 5:12; 23:29-31, 34, 37; Lk 6:23; 11:48; Acts 7:52; Rom 11:2-3; Heb 11:37.

In short, the typological relationship did not first consist in reasoning in terms of an announcement and a fulfillment but in making known the parallels that exist between Jesus and the prophets –

---

[12] Cf. Mt 16:4; 21:11, 46; Mk 6:15; 8:28; Lk 7:16; 24:19.

including John the Baptist, who himself was recognized as such by the crowds before and after his death[13]. Yet, the *synkriseis* established by the Synoptics between Jesus and the prophets from the past, based on literary indicators, cannot but be accepted by exegetes. That is why, even if one does not go as far as to reason in terms of announcement and fulfillment, one is authorized to speak of typology when the *synkriseis* have the role of making the prophetic being of Jesus known. In other words, it is the journey of the *anagnôrisis* in each Gospel that allows distinguishing from among the *synkriseis* those that are properly typological.

The number of *synkriseis* is, moreover, such that some have gone so far as to declare that Jesus did not exist and that the gospel writers had created a biographical work by going fishing in all the narratives of the Scriptures and with their help had created the character Jesus[14]. The present essay will not question the historical reliability of the typological *synkriseis* elaborated by the Synoptics. Let us only say, in a few words, that it is regrettable to pass forthwith from the *synkrisis*, a literary technique, to the negation of the historical reality. Rather than go towards the historical Jesus, the developments that follow will, moreover, have for a primary goal to say why the Synoptics could not do without *typology* in order to write their narratives and why the choice of the Old Testament types differ from one Synoptic to another.

III. AN ENIGMA OF THE TYPOLOGY OF THE SYNOPTICS

Traditionally, in the typological relationship, the old and new elements were respectively called announcement and fulfillment[15].

---

[13] Cf. Mt 11:9; 14:2, 5; 21:26 and parallels.

[14] Thus, for ex., T.L. BRODIE, *Beyond the Quest for the Historical Jesus*. Memoir of a Discovery, Phoenix Press, Sheffield, 2012.

[15] Also, *figura/veritas*; *umbra/veritas*; for the evolution of the appellatives over time, see E. AUERBACH, *Figura*.

By declaring that his Passion and his death had to fulfill the Scriptures (Mk 14:49), the Jesus of Mark confirms without any doubt the statement. But such a declaration is valid only because in each episode of the Passion there exists one or several motifs that repeat those of the supplications of the persecuted innocent – plot, betrayal, solitude, false accusations, etc. Furthermore, in the Passion narrative in Mark, these psalmic motifs are used for the *anagnôrisis*, as I have shown in *The Birth of the Gospels as Biographies*[16]. One can, henceforth, ask if the announcement/fulfillment relationship is necessarily a part of the topology of the gospel narratives. Typological rereading already existed in the Scriptures of Israel, and whatever may be said, it is not always oriented eschatologically or, said otherwise, from the less towards the more[17]. I hope, moreover, to show that in order to study the typology of the Synoptics it is today more exegetically useful to focus on the essential role that it has for the *anagnôrisis* of Jesus as prophet and, in the Passion narratives, as a persecuted innocent.

But if, as has been said since Saint Augustine[18],
Novum in Vetere latet,
Vetus in Novo patet,
it is, nevertheless, surprising that the Old Testament types appealed to in order to describe the identity of Jesus are in so many cases so difficult to detect; when the Synoptics proceed typologically, they allude to biblical characters from the past, without or rarely mentioning them, to the point that one could reverse the expression and say: Vetus in Novo *latet*. But, will one object, in Lk 4:25-27 Jesus does mention Elijah and Elisha, the two types beginning with which he is going to construct his prophetic typology. Undoubtedly, but

---

[16] *The Birth of the Gospels*, pp. 31-38.
[17] On the typology of the Holy Scriptures of Israel, see, in the final bibliography, the studies of M. Fishbane, P. Beauchamp, T. Römer, J.P. Sonnet.
[18] *Quaestiones in Heptateuchum*, 2:73: The New is hidden in the Old, the Old is revealed in the New.

thereafter, when in Lk 7:11-17 and 17:11-19 the narrator refers to the two prophets and, more precisely, to the episodes in 1 Kings 17 and 2 Kings 5[19], he does not mention them: there the typological reprise is entirely allusive. The observation is valid for the majority of these reprises in Luke, but also in Mark and Matthew, as we will see. Providing the reasons for which the typology of the Synoptics – in particular that in their Passion narratives – is predominantly allusive actually comes down to grasping its purpose.

One reason, pertinent but not decisive, can be provided. One indeed knows that at that time, it was customary to cite a phrase or two from a well-known author without mentioning him, leaving it to the reader to come up with his name. Even a cursory comparison with the *Chaereas and Callirhoe* by Chariton of Aphrodisias, written less than one hundred years after the Synoptics, is instructive, for, in this ancient novel, one notes more than twenty citations – one or two verses each – from the Iliad and the Odyssey, inserted into the text without any indication, Chariton only once mentioning the name of Homer; in 2:3: "Have you not heard what Homer taught us?", a question that illustrates two verses from the seventeenth book of the Odyssey. The statement is also valid for the author of Luke/Acts and, to a lesser extent, for Matthew and Mark[20]. But this is not the principal reason for which the typological reprises of the Synoptics can in general only be perceived by those who have a good knowledge of the Scriptures of Israel.

If the typological reprises of the Synoptics are so discrete, it is because in reality to recognize Jesus as a prophet and to believe in him is not self-evident: to the characters of the gospel narratives, but to the reader as well, some signs are provided by the typology, but, like all the signs, they are offered with discretion. This is really

---

[19] On these episodes, see *The Birth of the Gospels*. pp. 97-98 and pp. 100-102.
[20] Specialists have noted that the author of Luke/Acts proceeds in the same way. Cf. Chap. VII of this essay, "The Culture of the Narrator of Luke/Acts. From Techniques to Theology".

the paradox: typology is used by the narrators in order to help the narrative's characters and the reader recognize in Jesus a prophet and a persecuted innocent, but it itself is only recognized with difficulty. It is thus all the more urgent to help the readers grasp its importance and its real logic.

IV. CHANGING THE PARADIGM

For the reasons stated in the preceding paragraphs, the chapters that follow will not principally question the mysterious connection established by the Christian tradition between the two poles of the figure, between the type and the antitype, whether or not the type has wrongly been seen as a shadow of the later New Testament realities. That task, first and foremost, is for the specialists in the history of hermeneutics – in particular patristic and medieval. The exegete has, on the other hand, the duty to examine how the authors of the gospel narratives have proceeded and to show the pertinence of their typological reading in relation to the requisite of the recognition of Jesus as prophet, this primary *anagnôrisis* being in its turn necessary in order to give the reason for what was then considered as a contradiction and impossibility: the death on the cross of the Messiah.

CHAPTER II

THE TYPOLOGY OF THE SYNOPTIC GOSPELS
A PRELIMINARY OVERVIEW

With Synoptic typology being discrete, allusive, not all commentators are in agreement on the Old Testament figures appealed to and make pronouncements without necessarily making an argument. Actually, the methodological question is twofold. Before attempting to identify the Old Testament figures, it is important to show to which books, chapters or pericopae a passage from the Gospel narratives is possibly making an allusion. As Richard Hays says, it is important to note the Old Testament passages that the authors of the New are echoin[1]. The question on typology is only asked secondly, for all Old Testament allusions are not typological reprises.

The criteria for determining the scriptural echoes present in the Gospel narratives and the other New Testament writings not having been systematically identified, several recent studies have proposed to provide them, among others those of R. Hays, D.C. Allison and R. Knowles[2]. I am going to take up the presentation of the

---

[1] R. HAYS, *Echoes of Scripture in the Letters of Paul*, Yale University Press, New Haven, 1989, pp. 29-32. As P. FOSTER says, "Echoes without Resonance: Critiquing Certain Aspects of Recent Scholarly Trends in the Study of Jewish Scriptures in the New Testament", *JSNT* 38, 2015, pp. 96-97, instead of the word 'echo' that can indicate the involuntary reprise of a passage from the O.T., it is necessary to prefer 'allusion' that denotes a wanted reprise.

[2] HAYS, *Echoes of Scripture* (see the preceding note); D.C. ALLISON, Jr., *The New Moses*, A Matthean Typology, Fortress, Minneapolis, 1993, pp. 19-23; M. KNOWLES, *Jeremiah in Matthew's Gospel*, coll. JSNT Sup 68, Sheffield, 1993, pp. 162-222.

first two and briefly illustrate them with the help of one or two examples taken from the Synoptics.

I. ECHOES AND ALLUSIONS – THE CRITERIA

Richard Hays and Allusions to Scripture

Hays' essay treats the allusions made to Scripture by the apostle Paul, but the criteria that he provides are valid for the Synoptics. It suffices to replace the words 'Paul' or 'letters' with 'Synoptics' and to apply to the latter the rule, expressed in the form of a question.

(a) Did the Synoptics and their readers of that day have (or were they able to have) access to the biblical text that was being alluded to?

Three verses from the IIIrd Gospel, Lk 24:50-52, to which we will return at length in ch. V, can illustrate the question. They indeed seem to copy a passage from Sirach (50:20-21) describing the blessing given by the high priest Simon on the people gathered in the Temple[3]:

Sir 50:20-21	Lk 24:50-52
Then coming down he [the high priest Simon] would *raise his hands* over all the congregation of Israel, The *blessing* of the LORD would be upon his lips, the name of the LORD would be his glory. [21] they bowed down in *worship* a second time to receive the *blessing* of the Most High.	Then he [Jesus] led them [the disciples] out as far as Bethany, and *raising his hands* he *blessed* them. [51] While he *blessed* them, he parted from them. [52] And having *worshiped* him they returned to Jerusalem with great joy, and were continually in the temple *blessing* God.

At that time, all the Scriptures were not collected, like today, in one volume. If every synagogue had the scrolls of the five books

---

[3] The words in common to the two passages (to raise his hands, to bless/benediction, to worship) are in italics.

of the Torah, the Psalms, and the book of Isaiah, the other prophets and the books that today are called deuterocanonical, written in Greek, were found only in the wealthier synagogues of the Diaspora. Was the author of the IIIrd Gospel able to read Sirach? Do other passages from Luke allow giving an affirmative response to the question? If one believes some studies, Lk 12:19-20, close to Sir 11:19, seems to confirm the hypothesis[4].

(b) Is the verbal similarity easily identifiable, in other words does one find one or several words in common in the passages from the New Testament and the Old?

Undoubtedly, Lk 24:50-52 and Sir 50:20-21 have several words in common, as seen in the table.

(c) Is the same allusion identifiable in other passages of the same Gospel or elsewhere in the New Testament?

Luke 24:50-52 is the only passage in the New Testament where an allusion to Sir 50:20-21 is made.

(d) Is the highlighted scriptural echo in a thematic coherence with the moment of the Gospel narrative?

Exegetes for whom there is an allusion to Sir 50:20-21 in Lk 24:50-52 note that the recourse to a priestly context would form an inclusion with the first episode in Luke, located in the Temple in Jerusalem, an episode whose protagonist is a priest in the midst of officiating, Zachariah. The allusion to Sir 50:20-21 in Lk 24:50-52 would then emphasize the narrative coherence of the whole.

It is, nevertheless, necessary to note the important differences capable of counter-balancing a priestly interpretation: (i) if the high priest is in the Temple in order to bless the people at the end of the ceremony, Jesus and his disciples are not there; (ii) in Sirach 50 the

---

[4] Cf. A.G. MEKKATTUKUNNEL, *The Priestly Blessing of the Risen Christ*. An Exegetico-Theological Analysis of Luke 24,50-53, Peter Lang, coll. Europäische Hochschulschriften 714, Bern, 2001, pp. 191-192. Influenced by this thesis, F. BOVON, *L'évangile selon saint Luc*, Labor et Fides, Geneva, 2009, vol. IIId, p. 487, thinks as well that it is a priestly blessing.

people are not worshiping the high priest Simon, but God, whereas in Luke 24 it is Jesus who is the subject of the worship[5], as God.
(e) Would the readers at the time of the Synoptics be able to perceive the allusion (in view of their culture, etc.)[6]?

Perhaps it is useful to recall that individual reading was extremely rare and that the biblical books were read aloud in the assembly. Were there some believers with enough knowledge of the Scriptures and current literary models to explain the texts? What we know on the subject, unfortunately, does not allow us to respond with certitude.
(f) How many readers (from the first Fathers of the Church to today) have detected before us the scriptural allusion?

If one believes the specialists, Christian Antiquity does not seem to have commented on Lk 24:50-52. Bede, in the VIIIth century, would be the first to interpret in a priestly way Jesus' benediction[7].
(g) Does the presence of the highlighted allusion make sense, and does it clarify the passage of the Gospel that one is in the midst of reading?

If the benediction in Lk 24:50-52 is priestly, this means that henceforth Jesus is high priest, the one by whom and thanks to whom our prayers are presented to God. The Lucan narrator could not conclude his macro-narrative any better. This being said, it is necessary to choose between a high priest Jesus and a divine Jesus, worshiped as the Lord of glory.

What conclusions are authorized by the criteria proposed by Hays? The number of words in common in Lk 24:50-52 and Sir 50:20-21 clearly indicate an allusion to the priestly blessing at the end of celebrations. A passage from the Torah, Lev 9:22-24, where one finds the same vocabulary and the same background – the

---

[5] In Greek: *proskunèsantes auton*.
[6] Criterion called historical plausibility.
[7] *Expositio in Lucan*, VI,2393-2460. Cf. BOVON, *L'évangile selon saint Luc*, p. 493.

blessing of the people by the high priest Aaron – confirms the priestly denotation. And even if Luke is not alluding to Sir 50:20-21, he is describing, as was already done in Leviticus 9 and Sirach 50, the priestly blessing with words that had to be known by all Israelites – he is thus repeating a *topos*. But if the apostles worship Jesus resurrected, it becomes difficult to see in the character of the high priest, a man who for this reason cannot be worshiped, the figure of a Jesus henceforth Lord and whose glory is the same as God's. If then Jesus is not in the position of the high priest, why imply that his blessing is priestly or describe it as if it were? In spite of their pertinence, Hays' criteria do not authorize a solid response. Let us add that Lk 24:50-52, whose amphibology is well-known, is one of the passages where the list of criteria provided by Hays does not suffice.

Dale Allison's Criteria for Typological Allusions

If the criteria proposed by Hays have the goal of facilitating the pinpointing of the Old Testament allusions – and only this –, those of Allison, six in number, go further and are doubly interesting, for they present rules aimed at determining what is or is not typological and have, moreover, one of the Synoptics as their subject. I will illustrate these rules with the help of examples taken from Matthew, Mark, and Luke.

(*a*) The Old Testament echo is clear when a passage from the New explicitly mentions a character or event from the Old Testament.
So it is in Mk 9:11-13 where Jesus, alluding to John the Baptist, declares that Elijah of the end times has already come. Similarly, in Lk 4:25-27, Jesus describes his own ministry by explicitly referring to Elijah and Elisha.
This being said, the explicit announcements mentioned by Jesus or one of the Gospel writers are not all typological reprises.

In Mt 19:1-9 Jesus is explicitly referring to Gen 1:27 and 2:24[8], without it being necessary to see in this citation a figurative interpretation.

(b) A passage from the Old Testament can be repeated without an introductory formula. The scriptural echo is then clear.

On page 19 of his *New Moses*, Allison takes the example of Mk 1:6 where the narrator says of John the Baptist that he "had a leather girdle". This designation repeats exactly 2 Kings 1:18 (LXX), where this description allows the king Ahab to recognize Elijah.

The citation can as well be indirect, as known by all, as in Mt 12:7 where Jesus repeats Hosea 6:6 without naming it: "And if you had known what this means, 'I desire mercy, and not sacrifice,' etc.".

Let us lastly recall the cry of Jesus in Mt 27:46 "My God, my God, why hast thou forsaken me?" that is assuredly not preceded by an introductory formula.

(c) The circumstances being analogous, an event from the New Testament recalls one from the Old.

The most obvious example is found in Matthew 5–7 where Jesus' Sermon on the Mount clearly refers to the promulgation of the Law that Moses received from God on the mountain[9].

(d) If a passage from the New Testament repeats words or expressions from a passage from the Old, the allusion is possible, indeed probable.

Without there being a citation, Mk 6:36-44 repeats some of the words from the narrative of the multiplication of the loaves in 2 Kings 4:42-44, as the following table shows. The allusion is accepted by commentators[10].

---

[8] Gen 1:27: "Male and female he [God] created them"; Gen 2:24: "a man ... cleaves to his wife, and they become one flesh".

[9] On these chapters from Matthew, see ch. IV and ALLISON's study, *The New Moses*, pp. 182-194.

[10] Cf., for ex., J. MARCUS, *Mark 1-8*. A New Translation with Introduction and Commentary, Yale University Press, New Haven – London, 2008, p. 415; also,

	Mk 6:36-44	2 Kings 4:42-44
Jesus' and Elisha's Order	[37a] You give them (the crowds) something to eat	[42b 43b] give to the people that they may eat
Reaction of powerlessness	[37b] the disciples' objection	[43a] question from Elisha's servant
The amount of food	[38] five loaves (and two fish)	[42a] twenty loaves of barley
Consumption and leftovers	[42] they all ate and were satisfied [43] twelve baskets	[44a] they ate [44b] had some left
The number of guests	[44] 5000 people	[43a] 100 people

(*e*) If the narrative framework is similar in the two passages, there is a reprise.

As the preceding table shows, Mk 6:36-44 and parallels, where the plot progresses as it does in 2 Kings 4:42-44, once again excellently illustrate the criteria proposed here.

In order for a *synkrisis* to be declared as typology, this criterion is a necessary complement to the one on the vocabulary stated in (*d*). What is more, even if the two Old and New Testament pericopae have only a few words in common, the typological reprise must always be notable thanks to the similar unfolding of the plot and to the semantic parallels between characters. Is it thus for the episode in Nain (Lk 7:11-17), where the place, the circumstances and the actors differ partially from those in 1 Kings 17:17-24 and seem to go against criterion (*c*): in Zarephath, Elijah, the widow and her dead son find themselves alone in a house, whereas in Luke 7, everything happens outside, at the city gate, where a large crowd is

---

Camille FOCANT, *L'évangile selon Marc*, Cerf, coll. Commentaire biblique du Nouveau Testament 2, Paris, 2004, p. 251.

The observation is valid for Matthew and Luke, but also for Jn 6 that in v. 9 repeats the expression "barley loaves" from 2 Kings 4:42.

present at the miracle; and if the widow of Zarephath reproaches
Elijah for his having brought misfortune with him (v. 17), that of
Nain cries, without ever addressing Jesus. But if the place and the
circumstances seem to prohibit some kind of *synkrisis*, the sentence
"he [Jesus] gave him to his mother" and the semantic parallels between characters – the widows, the dead only sons, Elijah and Jesus
– invite, on the contrary, seeing in the episode of Nain a figurative
interpretation:

1Kings 17:17-24	Lk 7:11-17
the *widow* (v. 20)	a *widow* (v. 12)
her dead *son* (vv. 17, 20)	the dead only *son* (v. 12)
the child cried (v. 22)	the dead (child) began to speak (v.
[Elijah] *gave him to his mother* (v.	15)
23)	[Jesus] *gave him to his mother* (v. 15)
the widow's reaction (v. 24):	the reaction of all (v. 16):
"you are a man of God"	"a great prophet has arisen"

(*f*) When the order of the words from the passage from the
New Testament follows grosso modo that of the Old, there is probably an allusion.

The words that follow the progression of the Old Testament
narrative must clearly be essential to the plot. The preceding table
verifies the pertinence of the latter criterion provided by Allison.

The criteria of Hays and Allison are complementary. It is by
having them play together – and not separately – that exegesis can
identify with more probability a typological allusion. But, to note
an allusion does not suffice, for, even when it is easily identifiable,
interpreting it correctly remains, as Foster has noted regarding the
cry of Jesus in Mk 15:34: "My God, my God, why hast thou forsaken me?" (Ps 21/22:2)[11]. He indeed points out that all the interpretations of this cry are not compatible. Some see in it an appeal
in Jesus' dereliction, without there being more, whereas for others,
by saying these words, Jesus is wanting to point out that following
the psalmist, he is expecting divine help, certain that his cry will be

---

[11] FOSTER, "Echoes without Resonance", pp. 100-101.

heard. I have already explained this cry[12] and will come back to it in ch. III of the present essay.

What these criteria do not say is that even if a citation and an allusion are obvious, it remains to interpret their function, and generally that is where the difficulties begin. In his study on Jesus' entrance into Jerusalem (Mt 21:1-11), Nieuviarts notes that for all commentators the citation is that of Zech 9:9, but it is interpreted, to say the least, very diversely, which leads him to say[13]:

> If the power of the citation can be so great as to thus link itself to all its context, one must, using a rigorous method, be able to verify that the narrative programs – that is the syntax, the sequence of the narrative – are similar in both contexts: the one from which the citation is extracted and the one into which it is put. Such an identification can only take place with total rigor if the interpretation does not want to be mistaken or mad[14].

Let us add that the vocabulary is indicative of an allusion if and only if it is in combination with a semantic parallelism[15]. Thus, it is not because the adjective *mogilalos*[16] appears only in Is 35:6 and Mk 7:32 that the relationship is typological. The passage from Isaiah could indeed have said that God will render *mogilaloi* all men of haughty speech, all the 'great boasters'. It would then be difficult, indeed impossible, to say that Mk 7:32 alluded to that verse from the Old Testament. If one can say that Mk 7:32 alludes to Is 35:6, it is because a clear semantic parallelism exists between the

---

[12] ALETTI, *Birth*, pp. 33-34. A longer demonstration in ID., "De l'usage des modèles en exégèse biblique. Le cas de la mort de Jésus dans le récit marcien", in V. COLLADO BERTOMEU (ed.), *Palabra, prodigio, poesia*, FS Luis Alonso Schökel, coll. AnBib 151, Rome, 2003, pp. 337-348.

[13] J. NIEUVIARTS. *L'entrée de Jésus à Jérusalem* (Mt 21,1-17). Messianisme et accomplissement des Écritures en Matthieu, Cerf, coll. LD 176, Paris, 1999, p. 26.

[14] Similarly, p. 26: "A single word, a single figure does not in itself create a link between two narratives. The presence of one word, one figure, is not sufficient for recognizing an allusion".

[15] The same observation in FOSTER, "Echoes without Resonance", p. 109.

[16] Literally: "who speaks with difficultly", which means "almost mute".

two: the *mogilaloi* will be able (Isaiah) /were able (Mark) finally to cry out with joy and to proclaim the great deeds of God who causes mutes to speak and created all things new; the creative behavior of Jesus in Mk 7:31-37 is thus paralleled with that of YHWH in Is 35:3-10.

If a unique word does not suffice to corroborate an allusion, on the other hand, a unique semantic parallel certainly connotes one. If it is indeed accepted by commentators that in Matthew 2 the character Jesus has his type in Moses, it is because the single Old Testament narrative that we have of a guide and liberator of Israel recognized as the greatest by the tradition and threatened with death from his birth is that of Exodus 1–2. This being said, the Mosaic typology in Matthew 2 is confirmed by other passages from the same macro-narrative (Matthew 5–7, etc.). To the criteria stated by Allison, it is thus necessary to add the (*c*) of Hays, by modifying it substantially: a typological allusion (to Moses, to Elijah or another) is much more probable when others of the same nature exist in the macro-narrative. In *The Birth of the Gospels as Biographies*, I have, moreover, recalled, with several commentators, that prophetic typology – Samuel as a type of Jesus – covers Lk 1–2 in its entirety, not only because of Lk 2:40 and 52 whose words repeat grosso modo 1Sam 2:26[17] but also because the sole passage from the Scriptures describing the conception, the birth and the early childhood of a prophet is found in 1Sam 1–2 and that the remainder of the Lucan macro-narrative, where prophetic typology prevails, confirms that first *synkrisis*[18].

---

[17] 1 Sam 2:26: "Now the boy Samuel continued to grow both in stature and in favor with the LORD and with men"; Lk 2:40: "And the child [Jesus] grew and became strong, filled with wisdom; and the favor of God was upon him"; Lk 2:52: "And Jesus increased in wisdom and in stature, and in favor with God and man".
[18] ALETTI, *Birth*, pp. 91-93.

II. THE DEPLOYMENT OF THE TYPOLOGY

The principal criteria used to highlight the allusions to the Old Testament and the typological reprises having been briefly presented, it remains to point out, before returning to it in greater length over the course of the following chapters in order to make its goal known, how the Synoptics proceed in order to elaborate their figurative interpretation.

According to the Number of Figures

A macro-narrative can proceed by selection, by only placing Jesus in relationship with one or another character from the Old Testament. Thus, as one will see in ch. III, the Markan narrator only places Jesus in a typological relationship with the persecuted innocent of the supplications, and this in his narrative of the Passion. Some episodes, such as the first multiplication of the loaves (Mk 6:36-44) mentioned above, display, it is true, a prophetic typology – Elisha as a type of Jesus – but commentators admit that they are not from the narrator, but rather from his sources[19].

Unlike Mark, the Matthean narrator proceeds by the accumulation of figures, since, in order to describe the identity of Jesus, he refers to Moses (Matthew 2; Matthew 5–7; etc.)[20], to Jeremiah[21], and, during his narrative of the Passion, to the persecuted innocent of the supplications, like Mark[22].

According to the Stage of the Redaction

The case of Mark invites the exegesis to take into account the redactional layers. In this macro-narrative, the prophetic typology clearly makes Elijah the type of John the Baptist, a typology first

---

[19] Cf. *infra*, the paragraph on the redactional layers.
[20] Cf. ALLISON, *The News Moses*, *passim*.
[21] Cf. KNOWLES, *Jeremiah*, *passim*, which shows the importance of the Jeremian typology in Matthew.
[22] Cf. ALETTI, *Birth*, pp. 52-61.

stated by the narrator in 1:6, which describes him as the Elijah in 2 Kings 1:8 and which is confirmed by Jesus himself in 9:13. In short, in Mark, the typology of Elijah is focused on John the Baptist and not on Jesus, which the narrative of the call of the first four disciples in Mk 1:16-20 seems to contradict. That is why, according to several commentators, the presence of the typology of Elijah in this episode must come from a pre-Markan redaction. But, even if one adopts this hypothesis, it is important to ask why the narrator of the Markan macro-narrative judged it good to keep the multiplication of the loaves and other episodes with a typological resonance, and especially, for his narrative of the Passion, with massive recourse to typology, by making the persecuted innocent of the supplications the types of Jesus suffering and put to death[23].

The question is the same for the narratives of the miracles where one can discern a reprise of the typology of Elisha, which is not in contradiction to the preceding one, that of Elijah, to the extent that there the type is not Elijah but Elisha, who succeeded Elijah, as Jesus did John the Baptist. If these Old Testament allusions have the role of describing, based on his behavior, the identity of Jesus, they must, nevertheless, be located in reference to the overall Christology of Mark, according to which, being the Messiah and the Son of God par excellence, Jesus has no Old Testament type with which he may be compared because *for the unique there is neither preparation nor prefigurement.*

According to the Distribution of the Figures

When a typological reprise runs throughout all or almost all of a macro-narrative, as does the prophetic one in Luke[24], one says that it is continuous. When it is only present in a single episode or in a single section of the macro-narrative, as that of the persecuted innocent in the Passion narratives in Mark and Matthew[25], it is partial. It is also possible to encounter several typological reprises in

---

[23] Cf. ALETTI, *Birth*, pp. 35-40. Also, the next chapter of this essay.

[24] Cf. ALETTI, *Birth*, pp. 89-106.

[25] Cf. ALETTI, *Birth*, pp. 35-37 and 55-58.

the same section, a phenomenon that one could qualify as multiple typology. Thus, it is in the Passion narrative in Matthew where it is accepted that the model of the persecuted innocent of the supplications is accompanied with allusions to the fate of Jeremiah[26].

According to the Speakers

To declare that there is typology in a Synoptic episode is not very pertinent if one does not take into consideration the one who is stating it: the narrator, the crowds, the opponents, the disciples, Jesus, indeed God the Father. Are Jesus and the divine voice going in the same direction as the other characters, do they correct them or do they reject their typology?

Thus, in Mk 1:6 it is the narrator who designates John the Baptist with the traits of Elijah, and actually he is only following the divine oracle in Mk 1:2-3, where God declares to the Messiah that he will cause a messenger to proceed him, who assuredly is the Elijah of the end times. To these two speakers is added a third in Mk 9:13, Jesus, being quite as reliable as the first two. These three voices point out without a doubt that in Mark Elijah is really the type of John the Baptist. One then sees that the opinions reported in Mk 6:14-16 and 8:28 according to which Jesus would be the Elijah of the end times are baseless: upon the differing reliability of the speakers depends the solidity of a typological reprise[27].

In Luke 1–2, the narrator, as pointed out above, develops a prophetic typology, with Samuel as the type of Jesus, whereas the angelic voices repeatedly state a royal typology.

In the episode of Jesus' entrance into Jerusalem in Matthew 21, the royal typology is also stated by several voices: by the narrator, who invokes the Scriptures, by the crowds, but also, in advance through an indirect way by Jesus himself, who wants to enter into

---

[26] Cf. KNOWLES, *Jeremiah*, pp. 217-222. The observation is also valid for Jn 19, where Jesus on the cross is the pascal lamb, the New Temple, etc.

[27] On the question of Elijah in Mark, we will examine the position of Gerhard Dautzenberg and other German-speaking exegetes in ch. III.

the city seated on a beast of burden. In Mt 21:1-11, Jesus and the narrator are not the only ones to allude to the royal prefigurement; the crowds themselves recognize in Jesus their Messiah and acclaim him as such. In this passage, the typological reprise is clearly polyphonic.

According to the Addressees

Undoubtedly, all the typological reprises are made for the reader, and in the passages where they are from the narrator, their primary, indeed unique, addressee is the reader. Thus, the phrase "and Jesus gave him to his mother" in Lk 7:15, can be understood as an allusion to 1 Kings 17:23 only by the reader. But in several episodes, the typology also has for addressees the characters of the narrative, as in Mk 9:13, where Jesus makes known to the three disciples that John the Baptist was Elijah of the end times and that he himself is, consequently, the Messiah.

Those who followed and listened to Jesus are also addressed with typological declarations, as those of Mt 12:39-41 and parallels:

> An evil and adulterous generation seeks for a sign; but no sign shall be given to it except the sign of the prophet Jonah. [40] For as Jonah was three days and three nights in the belly of the whale, so will the Son of man be three days and three nights in the heart of the earth. [41] The men of Nineveh will arise at the judgment with this generation and condemn it; for they repented at the preaching of Jonah, and behold, something greater than Jonah is here.

Similarly, in Lk 4:25-27, Jesus describes, for the inhabitants of Nazareth, his ministry with the help of those of Elijah and Elisha.

According to Biblical References

The typological reprises carried out by the Synoptics are diverse. Some are from the Exodus (Moses, Israel in the desert), others are royal (David, Solomon), others are psalmic (persecuted innocent), most are prophetic (Elijah, Elisha, Jonah, Jeremiah, the Servant of YHWH). But one does not ever encounter in these narratives a patriarchal or priestly figure – as we will show, Lk 24:50-52 does not make Jesus a high priest. Exegesis must explain these choices.

III. THE STAGES OF THE ANALYSIS

The next chapters are respectively devoted to Mark (ch. III), Matthew (ch. IV) and Luke (ch. V). In each, we will begin by presenting a representative pericope from the macro-narrative and will collect the elements without which one is unable to speak either of allusion or figurement, namely the vocabulary and the semantic route that must be more or less the same in the pericopae of the New Testament and the Old. After having identified the types and the antitypes, it will remain to determine the *function* of the noted typology within the pericope being studied but also within the macro-narrative. A typological reprise indeed does not have, as will be seen, the same role if it is found at the beginning of a macro-narrative as it does if it is found at the end. The last chapter will return to the question of changing the paradigm.

CHAPTER III

CHRISTOLOGY AND TYPOLOGY
IN THE NARRATIVE OF MARK

This chapter's objective is to provide the reasons for which Mark has recourse to a typology of Elijah, but also to a typology of Elisha and, in his Passion narrative, to a psalmic typology.

I. JOHN THE BAPTIST AND THE TYPOLOGY OF ELIJAH

Mark 6:14-16 and 8:27-28

In Mk 1:6, the narrator, as well as the divine oracle in Mk 1:2-3 and the protagonist Jesus in Mk 9:11-13, implicitly make Elijah the type of John the Baptist. As these three voices are authoritative, there is no possible doubt about the pertinence of this typological reprise. But, in two other passages, Mk 6:14-16 and 8:27-28, the narrator echoes different opinions on Jesus and reports that, for some, he is Elijah.

Mk 6:14-16	Mk 8:27-28
King Herod heard of it; for Jesus' name had become known. Some said (Greek: *elegon*), "*John the baptizer* has been raised from the dead; that is why these powers	And Jesus went on with his disciples, to the villages of Caesarea Philippi; and on the way he asked his disciples, "Who do men say that I am?" [28] And they told him, "*John the Baptist*;

(Greek: *dynameis*) are at work in him." [15] But others said, "It is *Elijah*." And others said, "It is a *prophet*, like *one of the prophets* of old." [16] But when Herod heard of it he said, "John, whom I beheaded, has been raised (Greek: *egerthè*)."	and others say, *Elijah*; and others *one of the prophets*."

If one believes Dautzenber[1], the German-language commentaries have certainly asked why Mark – and the parallel passages in Mt 14:1 and Lk 9:7-9 – mentions multiple opinions that differ from his, but they are especially interested in the connection between the redaction and the earlier tradition. Their results, unfortunately, do not converge: for some Mk 6:14-16 and 8:27-28 reflect two independent traditions[2]; for others, the tradition was reworked by the Gospel writers[3]; for others, Mk 6:14-25 would be traditional and 8:27-29 redactional[4]; for others still, the two passages would be redactional[5]. Whether the passages are reprises from a prior tradition or written by the Gospel writers, they clearly relate opinions that from their point of view are false. But which ones are false and for which narrator? For all three, certainly, the one concerning the identification of Jesus with John the Baptist. And for Mark, it is as well the case for Jesus' identification with Elijah, if one keeps in mind that for the divine oracle of Mk 1:2-3, for the narrator in Mk 1:6 and for Jesus in Mk 9:11-13, the Elijah of the end times is John the

---

[1] G. DAUTZENBERG, "Elija im Markusevangelium", in F. VAN SEGBROECK (ed.), *The Four Gospels*, FS. F. Neirynck, coll. BETL 100, Leuven, 1992, vol. 2, p. 1078.

[2] R. PESCH, *Das Markusevangelium*, Freiburg, Herder, vol. I, p. 332; vol. II, p. 31.

[3] J. GNILKA, *Das Evangelium nach Markus*, Benziger, Zürich-Neukirchen, 1978-1979, vol. I, p. 244; vol. II, p. 11.

[4] J. ERNST, *Das Evangelium nach Markus*, Pustet, Regensburg, 1981, pp. 178 and 234.

[5] D. LÜHRMANN, *Das Markusevangelium*, Tübingen, 1977, p. 113 and 143. A position that was also that of F. NEIRYNCK, "KAI ELEGON en Mc 6,14" ETL 65, 1, pp. 110-118; DAUTZENBERG, "Elija im Markusevangelium", pp. 1078-1079.

Baptist. But it is not certain that for the Lucan narrator such an identification is erroneous, as we will see in ch. V[6].

The historian, it is true, before giving his opinion on the truth or falsity of the declarations concerning Jesus' identity, attempts to know from where they came: during his ministry, after his death/resurrection, or at the time of the early Church. As for the interpreter, he himself is more interested in the way in which the Gospel narrators construct their characters, in particular their protagonist, and for them Mk 6:14-16 but also Mk 8:27-29 are passages that denote the importance of the *anagnôrisis*: all the narrative's characters, from the noblest to the humblest, repeatedly wonder who Jesus is. As several narrative studies have already shown that the part of Mark which goes up to the episode at Caesarea Philippi has for its common thread the question of Jesus' identity, of the recognition of which he had to be the subject, there is no need to retrace a fully delineated route[7]. Thanks to these works, it is possible to affirm that if the narrators point out other opinions about Jesus, in particular the one that makes him the Elijah of the end times, they also do so, following the prophets and ancient Jewish writers who had announced an eschatological Elijah as mediator of salvation, in order to imply that Jesus' thaumaturgical behavior corresponded to the expectations[8].

In his article on Elijah in Mark, Dautzenberg asks if Mark and the other two mention the opinions of Herod and many others in order to show them to be erroneous and that their Christology is by far superior or in order to report the Christological positions that are in opposition to theirs. The narrative texture of Mark shows rather that the reason for which the narrator mentions opinions different

---

[6] Mt 14:1-5 does not mention Elijah.

[7] See in particular that of P. MASCILONGO, "*Ma Voi, chi dite che io sia?*" Analisi narrativa dell'identità di Gesù e del cammino dei discepoli nel Vangelo secondo Marco alla luce delle 'Confessione di Pietro' (Mc 8,27-30), GB Press, Rome 2011.

[8] Cf. Mal 3:1; 3:23-24; Sir 48:10. On the eschatological prophet, also see 1QS 9:11.

from his is something else: if he had not mentioned them, it would have simply signified that the *anagnôrisis* of Jesus had no importance whatsoever for him and for the characters of his narrative. Although insufficient, the typological reprise evoked in Mk 6:14-16 and 8:27-28 shows that it is the question of the *anagnôrisis* that moves Mark's narrative forward and that serves it.

Mk 6:17-29 Elijah and the Death of John the Baptist

[17] For Herod had sent and seized John, and bound him in prison for the sake of Herodias, his brother Philip's wife; because he had married her. [18] For John said to Herod, "It is not lawful for you to have your brother's wife." [19] And Herodias had a grudge against him, and wanted to kill him. But she could not, [20] for Herod feared John, knowing that he was a righteous and holy man, and kept him safe. When he heard him, he was much perplexed; and yet he heard him gladly.

[21] But an opportunity came when Herod on his birthday gave a banquet for his courtiers and officers and the leading men of Galilee. [22] For when Herodias' daughter came in and danced, she pleased Herod and his guests; and the king said to the girl, "Ask me for whatever you wish, and I will grant it." [23] And he vowed to her, "Whatever you ask me, I will give you, even half of my kingdom." [24] And she went out, and said to her mother, "What shall I ask?" And she said, "The head of John the baptizer." [25] And she came in immediately with haste to the king, and asked, saying, "I want you to give me at once the head of John the Baptist on a platter." [26] And the king was exceedingly sorry; but because of his oaths and his guests he did not want to break his word to her. [27] And immediately the king sent a soldier of the guard and gave orders to bring his head. He went and beheaded him in the prison, [28] and brought his head on a platter, and gave it to the girl; and the girl gave it to her mother.

[29] When his disciples heard of it, they came and took his body, and laid it in a tomb (Greek: *mnèmeion*).

After having pointed out the opinions of others on the identity of Jesus, the narrator recounts the occasion that precipitated the fate of the Baptist. Commentators have, of course, examined the reasons for this insertion, which, all things considered, has no impact whatsoever on the macro-narrative's plot. Marcus points out two[9]; the first, according to which this narrative would allow the disciples that were sent on a mission (Mk 6:7-13) to leave without having to return immediately (Mk 6:30ff.), is not significant, for already Mk 6:12-13 has summarily described the disciples' thaumaturgical activity to which the narrator has accustomed his readers from the beginning. The macro-narrative could have bypassed the death of the Baptist and conveniently gone from this summary (vv. 12-13) to the return of the disciples close to Jesus (v. 30). According to the second reason, qualified as "a deeper purpose" but which is also incorrect, by inserting the narrative of the decapitation of John the Baptist, the narrator wants to emphasize a paradox: "[t]he miraculous successes of the Christian missionaries are made possible by the suffering death of Jesus, to which the death of the Baptist points[10]". The narrator certainly parallels the deaths of the Baptist and Jesus, as the parallels in the table show:

Mk 6:17-29	Mk 14–15
Herod seized (*ekratèsen*) John the Baptist (6:17)	they seized (*ekratèsan*) Jesus (14:46)
he bound him (*edèsen*) (6:17)	
his disciples laid him in a tomb (*mnèmeion*) (6:29)	they bound (*dèsantes*) Jesus (15:1) Joseph laid Jesus in a tomb (*mnèmeion*) (15:46)

The narrator's intention is clear: by his death, the Baptist announces Jesus', quite as violent. In short, it is Christologically oriented. That a part of the disciples' thaumaturgical successes were owing to the salvific death of Jesus, one will willingly admit. But it is improbable that this episode was inserted for this reason, for (i) the death described in these verses is that of John the Baptist and not that of Jesus, (ii) the disciples' successes are described before our

---

[9] J. MARCUS, *Mark 1-8*. A New Translation with Introduction and Commentary, Yale University Press, New Haven-London, 2008, p. 397.
[10] MARCUS, *ibid*.

episode and without a link to it; indeed, the narrative of John's death
is not related to vv. 12-13 but to vv. 14-16 that immediately precede
it, as we are going to show.

If one pays attention to the narrator's way of proceeding, one
sees why he followed the various opinions on the identity of Jesus
with the narrative of the death of the Baptist. Indeed, vv. 14-16
prepare for vv. 17-29, as the following table shows:

Mk 6:14-16 **Erroneous Identifications** speakers = characters from the macro-narrative addressees = characters from the macro-narrative	Mk 6:17-29 **Correct Identifications** speaker = Markan narrator addressees = only the reader
Jesus = John the Baptist	vv.17-20 + 29 like John the Baptist, Jesus was arrested, bound, placed in a tomb
Jesus = Elijah	vv. 21-28 John the Baptist as Elijah threatened with death by the king's wife

The false opinions on Jesus serve as a springboard for the narrator who rebounds upon them in order to describe narratively the
relationships as he perceives them, between John the Baptist and
Jesus, between Elijah and John the Baptist, and to imply, once again,
that Elijah is the type of John the Baptist. Let us see how.

Several expressions from vv. 21-28 repeat word for word passages from the Book of Esther, as noted by commentators. King
Ahasuerus, being captivated by the beauty of Esther, a young Jewish
woman (*korasion*) who pleased him (*areskô*) to the point of his making her his wife[11], wants to satisfy a request that she dared to ask.
So, to gain her trust he declares to her: "What is your request? It
shall be given you, even to the half of my kingdom (*heôs hèmisous
tès basileias mou*)"[12]. In the same way, in Mark 6, after the young

---

[11] Est 2:9.
[12] Est 5:3; repeated in 7:2.

woman by her dance has pleased (*areskô*) Herod, he promises to grant her whatever she asks, "even half of my [his] kingdom (*heôs hèmisous tès basileias mou*, v. 23)". The vocabulary invites seeing in the Book of Esther the background of Mk 6:21-28. If this were so, the king Ahasuerus would be the type of Herod and Esther that of Herodias' daughter. It is necessary, however, to reject this inference, first because one cannot find in the Book of Esther a character capable of being the type of the Baptist. Moreover, if the vocabulary clearly indicates that the Markan narrator copied some expressions from the Book of Esther, this is not sufficient for speaking of a typological reprise. With the exception of beauty, Esther and Herodias' daughter have nothing in common: neither their status – the first is a queen but not the other –, nor their behavior – the first works for the life of her people, whereas the second asks for and obtains the head of John the Baptist.

So what to conclude? That these sentences really do come from the Book of Esther, for it is there and only there in Mk 6:21-28 that the same words are found. But there is not a semantic parallelism between the characters of the two narratives. This background is indeed neither the only one nor the most important. As commentators note[13], it is to the Elijah cycle that it is necessary to go in order to find situations and characters parallel to those in Mk 6:21-28. In both narratives, the three characters respectively have identical statuses:

	1 Kings 19:1-2	Mk 6:19, 21-28
king	Ahab	Herod
wife of king	Jezebel	Herodias
prophet	Elijah	John the Baptist

In each narrative, the prophet is threatened with death by the wife of the king. That Mk 6:19 alludes to 1 Kings 19, there can be no doubt, for Jezebel is the only woman and the only queen of whom it is said in the Scriptures that she wanted to put to death a prophet.

---

[13] Cf., for ex., MARCUS, *Mark*, p. 400.

In addition to these characters of the same status and this dramatic situation, the two narratives have several semantic traits in common. (i) The two kings are in an abnormal marital situation: Ahab married a non-Israelite idolater and himself became one (1 Kings 16:31), about which the Deuteronomist narrator (Dtr) comments thus: "Ahab did evil in the sight of the LORD…" (1 Kings 16:30). As for Herod, he married Herodias, the wife of his brother, thus finding himself in a situation opposed to the Law and the will of God[14]. (ii) They are both weak, manipulated by their wives (1 Kings 21:7, 25; Mk 6:26). (iii) As for the two prophets, they do not hesitate to criticize their respective kings and to recall them to their duty (1 Kings 18:16-19, 21; Mk 6:18).

Verses 17-29 from Mark 6 thus have the role of correcting the false identifications stated in vv. 14-16 by the characters in the narrative and of formulating indirectly the true ones, those of the narrator: Jesus is neither Elijah nor the Baptist, for it is the latter two who are in a typological relationship. One must thus note the coherence of the typological writing of the narrator of Mark who, from the beginning of his macro-narrative, implies that Elijah is the type of the Baptist! As this narrator proceeds by accumulation, one may legitimately ask if two other passages must not be added to those already noted[15]: Mk 1:5 where John baptizes in the Jordan, on the banks of which begin and end the acts of Elijah[16], and, clearly, Mk 6:14-29.

Who is the addressee of this figurative interpretation? The reader alone, clearly. The narrator is implying that all question the identity of Jesus but remain far from the reality. Misunderstanding the identity of Jesus, they do not manage to go further than formulating that of John the Baptist. In Mark, the question of the

---

[14] Cf. Lev 18:16; repeated in Lev 20:21. Herodias, daughter of Herod the Great, was the niece of Herod Antipas, as she had been the niece of her first husband. But John the Baptist does not accuse Herod Antipas of having married his niece but rather the wife of his brother.
[15] Cf. above, Mk 1:2, 3, 6; 9:11-13.
[16] Cf. I Kings 17:3, 5 and 2 Kings 2:6-7.

figurative interpretation is located thus at the extradiegetic level, of the Gospel writer to the reader.

The narrative of the death of John the Baptist points out as well that henceforth the Elijah of the end times, who in the oracle of Mal 3 and the praise of Sir 48 was not described as a suffering and persecuted figure, becomes one.

A Model of Elijah for Jesus?

The passages presented up to now have highlighted the coherence of the typological writing in Mark for whom Elijah is the type of John the Baptist. One episode, in spite of everything, seems to be an exception, that of the call of the first four disciples in Mk 1:16-20, about which several commentators say that it finds its model in the call of Elisha by Elijah (1 Kings 19:19-21)[17]. These are the parallels noted by exegetes[18]:

	1 Kings 19:19-21	Mk 1:16-18 and 19-20
Elijah passes by where Elisha is Jesus passes by where the fishermen are	Elijah finds Elisha and passes close to him	in passing, Jesus sees Simon and Andrew + James and John

Call
  gesturing (Elijah)
  laconic (Jesus)
	Elijah casts his mantle on Elisha
	(meaning: Elisha must accompany him and succeed him)
		Jesus: "Follow me"
		+ v. 20

Quick response (Elisha)	Elisha: "I will follow you" (akoloutheô)	They followed him (akoloutheô)

---

[17] Thus B.M.F. VAN IERSEL, *Mark. A Reader-Response Commentary*, coll. JSNT Sup Series 164, Sheffield, 1998, p. 128; MARCUS, *Mark 1-8*, p. 179, 181 (on the verb to call, in Greek: *kalein*).

[18] MARCUS, *Mark 1-8*, p. 183; A.Y. COLLINS – H.W. ATTRIDGE, *Mark*, Fortress, coll. Hermeneia, Minneapolis, 2007, p. 157, also mention a narrative of a Greek call in Pseudo-Diogenes (38:4-5), according to which the one who the philosopher called the next day distributes his goods to his family and follows him.

immediate (the four fishermen)	"he went after Elijah"	+ v. 20 "they followed him"

In light of these resemblances, what to conclude? If one believes some of the commentaries, "the point of this parallel is not that Jesus is Elijah (cf. 6:15; 8:28); that role is assumed in Mark's Gospel by John the Baptist (cf. 1:2-8; 9:11-13)…"[19] But the difficulty remains, for, if for the rest of the Markan macro-narrative, Elijah is in fact the type of only Jean the Baptist, why is the call of Mk 1:16-20 so close to that of 1 Kings 19:19-21, the sole passage from the Old Testament where a prophet indicates to someone he encounters to follow him without vacillating, to leave everything, property and family, in order to become his disciple[20]? In 1 Kings 19 and in Mark 1, neither Elijah nor Jesus introduce themselves and seemingly neither Elisha nor the four fishermen state their names. Only the call and the immediate positive response are kept.

If one examines the two passages more closely, an important difference, nevertheless, exists between them. For in 1 King 19, it is not Elijah who chose Elisha as successor, *but YHWH Himself* (1 King 19:16). Elijah only executes the order that was given to him with a gesture[21], whereas in Mk 1:16-20, it is Jesus who by his own authority calls those whom he wants for disciples. If Mk 1:16-20 uses the narrative model in 1 Kings 19:19-21, the characters Elijah and Jesus are not for all that parallel, and one must then exclude any typological reprise[22].

---

[19] MARCUS, *Mark 1-8, ibid.*

[20] The question of being able to take leave of his parents before following Elijah must be interpreted positively: Elisha shows that he takes seriously the commandment of the Decalogue concerning parents; he is thus faithful to the Law and for this reason reliable. By adding that he leaves everything, the narrative points out that he has truly seen how radical the call of Elijah was.

[21] A narrative analysis of 1 Kings 19:19-21 is here excluded, but one can affirm without error that the prophet's silence is aimed at showing the reader that the initiative of the call does not come from him.

[22] Other passages from Mark have been considered as making Elijah the type of Jesus. Thus, for ex., the latter's time in the wilderness (Mk 1:12-13) and that of

From the preceding paragraphs, it is possible to draw three conclusions. The first is methodological: the reprise of a literary model does not necessarily denote a typological relationship. The other two, semantic: in Mark the typology of Elijah has for its anti-type John the Baptist and him alone; and if he is the Elijah of the end times, it is because Jesus is the Messiah.

II. JESUS AND THE TYPOLOGY OF ELISHA

Even if in Mark Elijah is only the figure of John the Baptist, the prophetic typology is not limited to these two characters. Does not Jesus himself state obliquely in Mk 6:4 that he is a prophet[23]? The episode of the multiplication of the loaves, where the allusion to 2 Kings 4:42-44 is certain, as was seen in ch. II, also seems to make Elisha the type of Jesus[24]:

	Mk 6:36-44	2 Kings 4:42-44
Jesus' and Elisha's order	37a You give them (the crowds) something to eat	42b 43b Give to the men that they may eat
Reaction of powerlessness	37b the disciples' objection	43a question of Elisha's servant
The amount of food	38 five loaves (and two fish)	42a twenty loaves of barley
Consumption	42 they ate and were satisfied	44a they ate
Leftovers	43 twelve baskets	44b there was some left
The number of guests	44 5000 people	43a 100 people

Elijah at the brook of Cherith (1 Kings 17:1-6). But the parallels between these two passages are nonexistent.

[23] Mk 6:4: Jesus said to them: "A prophet is not without honor, except in his own country, and among his own kin, and in his own house."

[24] For a complete account of the parallels between 2 Kings 4:42-44 and Mk 6:36-44, see J.M. VAN CANGH, La multiplication des pains et l'eucharistie (LD 86), Paris, 1975, pp. 65-66.

For there to be a typological reprise, in addition to the vocabulary – loaves, to eat –, the parallelism between the plots and the characters is necessary. And yet, in 2 Kings 4 and in Mark 6, the complication comes from the orders of Elisha and Jesus, who respectively invite the servant and the disciples to feed a crowd with practically nothing. The reaction of powerlessness by the servant and the disciples causes the suspense to grow in 2 Kings 4 and in Mark 6. But Elisha and Jesus know that they can feed the crowd, and this happens. Both episodes emphasize the protagonists' thaumaturgical power. In short, the semantic parallelism between Elisha and Jesus invites interpreting their relationship figuratively. Let us recall that a typology of Elisha does not clash with that of Elijah, between Elijah and John the Baptist, for Elisha succeeded Elijah, as Jesus did John the Baptist. But if the typological relationship is noted so easily, its role remains more difficult to determine. As no reaction of those who ate is pointed out – neither an oral appreciation nor a praise-filled recognition –, the *anagnôrisis* is only required by the reader.

The reader must indeed understand, thanks to episodes like the multiplication of loaves, where the typology of Elisha occurs, that by coming after the Elijah of the end times, Jesus brings to an end the series of prophetic figures. It must still be asked why, in Mk 6:44, the satisfied crowds do not praise their benefactor – in the Markan narratives of miracles, the *anagnôrisis* of the crowds is lacking or remains indistinct, as in Mk 2:12 and 5:20[25]. Most of the characters of the Markan narrative never come to recognize and confess Jesus as the Messiah and Son of God. And if the disciples will manage to do so (Mk 8:29), the narrator recalls that they, nevertheless, did not understand the Christological impact of the multiplication of the loaves (Mk 6:52; 8:17-21). *In illo tempore*, neither the crowds nor the disciples were able to achieve a perfect *anagnôrisis*, which, on the other hand, ought to be the reader's. For by explicitly pointing out to him that the multiplication of the loaves and the walking upon the water must be read together in order to be able to

---

[25] Mk 2:12: "We never saw anything like this!"; 5:20: "all men marveled."

identify Jesus correctly (Mk 6:52), the narrator does not refer his reader only to the miracles of Elisha[26]. He is implying that Jesus is, like YHWH during the Exodus, capable of satisfying his people and controlling the waves, in other words: creator and master of the elements. The point here is still that of the (divine) authority of Jesus, as in the episode of the call of the first four disciples.

The reader will have sensed that the utilization that Mark makes of Elisha is paradoxical, for his figurative reading goes beyond the Elisha/Jesus *synkrisis*. Elisha's deed, which itself is fed by the exodic model[27], actually serves in Mark to show that Jesus is invested with the creative power of God. This is the paradox: supported by the *synkrisis* between type and antitype, this typology, essentially dual, goes beyond itself, towards Jesus, a unique figure.

III. JESUS AND THE PSALMIC TYPOLOGY

During the narrative of Jesus' ministry, different characters question his identity without ever arriving at a satisfactory recognition. This observation is valid for the disciples, for if they confess that Jesus is the Messiah, they see in him only the glorious king of the end times, and Jesus must correct this unilateral representation (Mk 8:31-33). With the narrative of his Passion and death, any real recognition by the characters is in the end excluded. Not that the recognition of Jesus' identity is not of decisive importance, much to the contrary, as the sessions before the Sanhedrin and Pilate, and especially the provocations at the foot of the cross, indicate, but it is the definitive rejection by all categories of the people that prevails.

The absence of a final horizontal *anagnôrisis* seems to undermine the Markan Passion. But the death of Jesus is followed by his resurrection, by which the mocked crucified one receives from God

---

[26] The crossing of the Jordan (2 Kings 2:7-8, 14-15) and the multiplication of the loaves (2 Kings 4:35-40).

[27] A point emphasized by recent commentators (Marcus, Collins, etc.).

the greatest recognition, that of glory and universal lordship. Being vertical, does the divine *anagnôrisis* dispense with a horizontal *anagnôrisis*? In other words: Why did Mark systematically exclude from the end of his narrative any horizontal recognition – including the disciples'[28]?

Let us not forget that, at that time, a biography (*bios*) could only be of illustrious men. Exactly what Jesus could not be, given his ignominious death and the rejection of which he was still the object when the Markan narrator wrote his narrative. The genius of this narrator was to have recourse to a biblical model, that of the supplications of the persecuted just, thanks to which he showed that having lived the same torments and rejections as the innocent of the psalms, Jesus had only to be recognized *by God alone*. The persuasive power of his narrative of the Passion comes from each episode taking up (at least) one motif of these supplications and from the progressive construction of a *synkrisis* that identifies Jesus and the persecuted faithful of the psalms.

The Persecuted Just of the Psalms, Types of Jesus

In *The Birth of the Gospels as Biographies*, I have shown that the Passion narrative of Mark was watered by psalmic typology, the persecuted just of the supplications being the type of Jesus suffering and dying on the cross[29]. Here, for the record, I will recall the principal motifs:

Anointing at Bethany

	Passages from Mark	**Passages of Supplications**
plot stated by the Nr	14:1-2	Ps 30/31:14; 40/41:8-9; 63/64:5-7; 70/71:10-11
betrayal announced by the Nr	14:10-11, 20-21	Ps 40/41:10

Jesus' Last Supper with the Disciples

---

[28] Later we will return to the centurion's declaration in Mk 15:39.

[29] ALETTI, *Birth*, pp. 33-38.

betrayal announced by Jesus	14:17-21	Ps 40/41:10
Jesus' announcement of the disciples' flight	14:26-31	Ps 30/31:12,11; 87/88:19

Gethsemane
Jesus' Prayer vv. 32-42

prayer spoken by Jesus	14:32b	Ps 108/109:4
condition of Jesus' spirit stated by Jesus	14:34	Ps 41/42:6, 12; 42/43:5; 54/55:3, 5; 37/38:11; 108/109:21/22
supplication stated by Jesus	14:36	Ps 88/89:27; 39/40:8
handing over to sinners Jesus' statement to the disciples	14:41	Ps 139/140:5; 87/88:9

The Arrest vv. 43-52

the disciples' flight told by the Nr	14:50	Ps 30/31:12/11; 87/88:19
Peter's denial said by Peter and the Nr	14:54 "at a distance"	Ps 37/38:12 the same adverbial expression, *apo makrothen* = "at a distance"

The Trial
Before the Sanhedrin vv. 14:59-72

plot to condemn told by the Nr	14:55	Ps 36/37:22; 108/109:2; 30/31:14
false testimony told by the Nr and characters	14:57	Ps 34/35:11
Jesus's silence told by the Nr	14:60	Ps 38/39:10
insults told by characters and the Nr	14:65	Ps 68/69:8

Before Pilate

insults told by the Nr and the soldiers	15:16-20	Ps 68/69:8

The Death on the Cross vv. 15:1-37

drawing of lots for the clothes told by the Nr	15:24	Ps 21/22:19
mockery by opponents said by the characters	15:29-34	Ps 43/44:15-16
they shake their heads told by the Nr	15:29	Ps 21/22:8
they tempt Jesus told by the Nr and the characters	15:30-31	Ps 21/22:9; 70/71:11
"are you the Christ" said by the characters	15:32	Ps 88/89:39, 52
final cry of Jesus	15:34	Ps 21/22:2
gesture of the soldier with the vinegar told by the Nr	15:36	Ps 68/69:22

The allusions are truly made for the reader alone, for, as one will have perhaps noted, except for Jesus[30], the characters of the narrative do not know that they are living the drama described in the supplications: even those who are at the foot of the cross and mock Jesus are not aware of playing the role of the enemies of God; they are even convinced of the contrary, whereas, for the just of the supplications, their enemies are also and more importantly enemies of God.

The Logic of the Recourse to the Supplications

The correspondences between the supplications of the persecuted just and the Markan Passion narrative are neither occasional nor fortuitous. To show this, it suffices to consider the scenes at the

---

[30] Affirmations that find confirmation in Mk 14:21 and 49.

foot of the cross. There Mark takes up the progression of Ps 21/22 by reversing it. For, if the supplications begin with the cry from the psalmist in order to then state the reasons,

cry	"call for help", "to God, my cry", "God come to my help", etc.
reasons	the enemies want the ruin of the faithful
	they plot, weave their nets, snickering, etc.
	God is the only one able to save the just from death

in the narrative, the cry/reasons components must be reversed,

reasons	the enemies of the protagonist
	want his ruin and plot against him,
	they accuse him, condemn him
	and take him to a place of torture
cry	for this reason, the just turns toward God by crying:
	"God, come to my help", etc.

That is why in Mark the scenes at the foot of the cross take up in reverse order the motifs of Ps 21/22:

Ps 21/22 = supplication	Mc 15 = narrative
(a) appeals to God (v. 2)	(b) the causes that justify the cry:
(b) the causes that justify the cry:	actions: garments divided (v. 24b)
words: insults (v. 8f)	words: insults (v. 29b)
actions: garments divided (v. 19)	(a) Jesus appeals to God (v. 34).

The order had to be inverted, for the supplication begins with the cry (a) and only afterwards states the motivations, namely the mortifying situation of the supplicant (b); whereas, in the narrative, the enemies' actions and words (b) have the effect of provoking the reaction of the one who is attacked, Jesus (a).

The disposition of the scenes at the foot of the cross authorizes concluding that the preceding episodes, since the Last Supper, have the function of accumulating the reasons that lead to Jesus' cry: being the object of a plot, betrayal, false accusations, insults, placed on a cross, he is finally addressing God by repeating the words of

the persecuted psalmists. The numerous semantic parallels show
that a typological relationship exists between the supplicants of the
psalms and Jesus[31]. The typology has not only determined the
choice of the episodes and the scenes, it has as well allowed describing the drama lived by Jesus, following the example of the supplicants of the psalms. For, in the supplications, the innocent threatened with death is recognized by no one; all his friends, and seemingly God Himself, have abandoned him. The model taken up by
the narrator prohibits the protagonist Jesus from being recognized
by the other characters of the narrative, for the non-recognition by
all the other characters is an integral part of the model.

The Markan narrator shows that there was no final recognition
on the part of the other human actors because there did not have to
be one. He overcame the difficulty by emphasizing that Jesus, being
in the same situation as the innocent of the supplications, could not
and must not be the object of human recognition, and thus, his narrative could not end with such a recognition. In Mark, as in the Old
Testament model followed, it is not the human characters who determine the value and the status of the protagonist, but God alone.
The narrator of Mark has thus found a model where the final recognition of the human characters has no raison d'être. In fact, the Markan narrative does not end with the rejection of Jesus' coreligionists.
From the mouth of the young man, a divine herald, the divine recognition, the only one of value, has really taken place since Jesus was
raised from the dead, as announced by the young man in Mk 16:6-
7. The final recognition is thus really there. The genius of Mark is
not to have eliminated it, but, thanks to the model chosen to characterize the whole of his characters, that of the supplications of the
persecuted innocent of the psalms, he has done it by passing over
the human characters (a horizontal recognition, essential according
to the Greek canons) to the divine character (a vertical recognition).

---

[31] The typological relationship does not prohibit there being differences between
the figures (the types) of the psalms and the Jesus who is figured (the antitype).
Thus, the request for the total destruction of the enemies that is encountered in
some of these supplications (cf. Ps 16/17:13; 27/28:4; 30/31:18-19; 34/35:3-8;
58/59:14; 69/70:3-4; 140/141:7, 10) is, of course, not spoken by Jesus.

The Cry of Jesus[32]

An Appeal for Help

In *The Birth of the Gospels as Biographies*, I have several times stated that one could not correctly interpret Jesus' cry in Mk 15:34 if one separated it from the model to which it belongs[33]. My position has not changed, but here I have the occasion to clarify it.

As Mark faithfully follows the model of the supplications of the persecuted just, it is first of all necessary to recall that the initial cry is an appeal for help. If the one who is praying addresses his cry to God, it is that he expects from Him a prompt intervention because death is near. The cry certainly comes from a real dereliction – "a complete state of abandonment and moral solitude", as defined by dictionaries –, but the latter is not expressed in the cry, but rather in the reasons that accompany it. The cry is a request for help and salvation addressed to God. If, moreover, the supplicant calls out, it is because he hopes to receive from God help. It would be incoherent to address oneself to God if one hoped to receive nothing from Him. The cry thus in no way denotes despair[34].

The Certainty of Salvation?

But because he takes up Ps 21/22 – "My God, my God, why hast thou forsaken me?" – the appeal seems to be colored by a reproach that one finds in other psalms: "My God, be not deaf,", "be not silent", "be not far"[35]. The one who is praying is, moreover,

---

[32] For a *status quaestionis* on the interpretation of Jesus' cry from the cross, see H.J. CAREY, *Jesus' Cry from the Cross*. Towards a First-Century Understanding of the Intertextual Relationship between Psalm 22 and the Narrative of Mark's Gospel (LNTS 398), London – New York, T&T Clark, 2009, pp. 1-28.

[33] ALETTI, *Birth*, pp. 36-37.

[34] For Carey, by his cry, Jesus is asking God to give him justice rather than expressing his distress. The model very faithfully followed by the Markan narrator requires not separating the two points of view.

[35] Cf. Ps 27/28:1; 34/35:22; 38/39:13; 82/83:2; 108/109:1.

able to say "Do not be deaf!" if and only if he has incessantly called and if the dereliction lasts for a long time. And he can make re-proaches only if he himself is faithful. That is why for most of the individual supplications, those who are praying say that they are in-nocent, that God was "always their God" (Ps 21/22:10). Is Jesus thus reproaching God for having abandoned him?

To declare that God delays in intervening can lead the ill-treated and persecuted innocent to ask if God still counts him among His faithful, He who has promised to come to their aid. If He does not come to his help, could this not be because He no longer con-siders him as such? One could object that the question "My God, why have you abandoned me?" denotes a wavering faith. But not at all: this appeal for help shows, on the contrary, a faith that can no longer rely on the certitude of the nearness of God, a faith that hopes against all hope.

In Mk 15:34 the Greek words that formulate the question are *eis ti*, which one may translate: "To what end?". Jesus would then be asking God to make known to him the purpose of the abandon-ment in which He has left him. This reading changes nothing about the problem: the supplicant is ignorant of the ways of God; if God does not come to help, when He, moreover, declares that He protects from danger those that are faithful to him[36], the drama of the just becomes a divine drama[37]. In some supplications, it is true, the one praying who expects the divine help declares the certainty that his appeal will be heard, that it has even been granted[38]. Ps 21/22 end-ing with a thanksgiving for the help received (vv. 23-32) has caused a few commentators to say that by saying the first words of the psalm, Jesus meant to indicate that he would certainly be helped, and praised God for having brought about his salvation. One can-not, however, interpret the cry of Jesus in Mk 15:34 in relation to

---

[36] Cf., for ex., Ps 90/91 in its entirety.

[37] Let us additionally not forget that the *eis ti* is explicitly presented by the nar-rator as a translation of the Aramean *Imh*, which must, moreover, prevail over the translation that engenders the misunderstanding between *Eli* ('my God') and Elijah (the prophet).

[38] Cf., for ex., Ps 27/28:6-8.

only Ps 21/22 for the psalmic motifs from the narrative of the Markan Passion – plot, betrayal, abandonment by friends, false accusations, etc. – are far more numerous than those enumerated in this psalm. It is actually all the supplications of the persecuted just that are taken up by Mark, as if in the Passion of Jesus is implied the dereliction of all the innocents from the biblical past.

It is thus necessary to interpret Jesus' cry in relation to all the supplications of the persecuted just. Yet, in these supplications, if the appeals for help are addressed to God, it is so that He may respond. Similarly, the descriptions of the dereliction in which those who are praying find themselves have the function of recalling God to the urgency and the validity of the appeal. The two interpretations proposed above thus do not exclude each other: the one who is praying cries out in order to speak of his suffering but also because he hopes for the salvation of God. Because he has faithfully constructed his narrative of the Passion on the model of these supplications, the narrator Mark gives to Jesus' cry this double connotation.

The *anagnôrisis* and the Centurion's Declaration

The model of the supplications of the persecuted just followed by Mark for the Passion, as stated above, allowed excluding any horizontal *anagnôrisis*. The centurion's declaration, in Mk 15:39 "Truly this man was a Son of God", nevertheless, seems to contradict the proposal.

Recently, it is true, the verse has no longer been read as a confession of faith but as a statement that is rather aggressive, indeed ironic. The narrator indeed says that the centurion is "facing" (in Greek, *ex enantias*) Jesus. Yet, in the biblical Greek, the phrase *ex enantias* followed by the genitive is almost always used in battle narratives[39]; and one has for this reason thought "the spatial description of the centurion as standing opposite Jesus (*ex enantias*

---

[39] Around 50x. Ex 14:2, 3; Jos 8:11, etc.

autou), if it has any symbolic or metaphorical force at all, may well signify the initial role of the centurion as an enemy of Jesus or as one who afflicts him"[40]. As was said in the preceding chapter, it is important to use the vocabulary with the greatest prudence. Of course, the centurion, being a soldier and having very probably been present at the scourging, can have a bellicose reaction to the death of Jesus and consider that it was a deserved death, his declaration must then be read as an antiphrasis. This being said, an examination of the immediate literary context is not superfluous. Before the centurion's reaction, Mark has indeed inserted a statement on the curtain of the temple: "And the curtain of the temple was torn in two, from top to bottom" (Mk 15:38). With the centurion being more than five hundred meters from the sanctuary and not having been able to be present at the phenomenon, the information is clearly made for the reader alone. On the other hand, the statement in v. 39 does not refer to the curtain that was torn but to what the soldier saw, as the narrator notes: "And when the centurion, ..., saw (Greek: *idôn*) that he [Jesus] thus (*houtôs*) breathed his last". But as his declaration is preceded by the information about the curtain, the reader must interpret it in relation to this event[41]. The complete tearing of the curtain that prohibited entrance into the Holy of Holies symbolizes the free access of all to God: all henceforth may know Him, thanks to the death of Jesus on the cross. All, that is to say the pagans as well. It is because Jesus died that God is henceforth accessible to all and that the pagan centurion can be the first to say what he says. But the reader must also understand that in saying this, it is in front of God Himself that the centurion finds himself, even without knowing it.

The centurion's declaration is and must be a confession, an *anagnôriris*. But it alone does not suffice for responding to the

---

[40] COLLINS – ATTRIDGE, *Mark. A Commentary on the Gospel of Mark*, Fortress, coll. Hermeneia, Minneapolis, 2007, p. 765.

[41] On this verse, see B K. GAMEL, *Mark 15:39 as a Markan Theology of Revelation*, T&T Clark, coll. LNTS 574, Bloomsbury, 2017, in particular pp. 69-114. For this author, it is the mention of the tearing of the curtain that provides the key to reading the statement in v. 39 (pp. 87ff).

requirements that the Greeks imposed for *bioi*. For the centurion is alone, anonymous and a foreigner. His confession was in no way shared by the Israelites of Judea and the Diaspora of that time. Limited and inchoative, it, nevertheless, highlights the first effect of Jesus' death, namely the future recognition of the pagan nations.

Typology and *anagnôrisis*

The studies on New Testament typology in general say that the antitype Jesus leads to perfection what was carried out and lived by the Old Testament types. But assuming that typology is present, this connotation is not dominant in Mark's Passion narrative: there it does not say that Jesus' cry and sufferings bring to their perfection those of the supplications of the persecuted just. For, in this narrative, the primary role of the typology is to meet the challenge of the *bioi* of that time, in other words, to show that, even if he died on the cross, Jesus was, nevertheless, worthy of the highest recognition, that of God, and that a horizontal recognition, by his coreligionists and a fortiori by foreigners, was not a pertinent and essential criteria for determining the excellence of his character.

IV. CONCLUSIONS

When the Markan narrator recounts the miracles of Jesus by having recourse to typology, he, as we have seen, refers rather to Elisha, and indirectly to the "signs and wonders" effected by God during the Exodus. One can consequently ask why he did not emphasize, as will Matthew and Luke, the fact that being a prophet, Jesus could only have been, like the prophets, rejected and put to death by his coreligionists. Like the two other Synoptics, Mark could have then shown, that, far from being counterproductive, the rejection and death undergone by Jesus really served, on the contrary, his identification as a prophet. If he did not do this, it is clearly in order not to follow those who identified Jesus with Elijah, this

prophet being for him the type of only John the Baptist. And if neither Elijah nor Elisha knew the painful death of most prophets, it
was necessary for him to find another model to narrate the Passion.

Typology was thus necessary in order to respond to the scandal of a Messiah dying on a cross and to an impossible *anagnôrisis*.
In other words, without recourse to typology, the Markan narrator
would never have been able to write a life (*bios*) of Jesus. All this
is played out in the Passion narrative and the death on a cross. During his ministry, Jesus had been identified by the crowds with Elijah
or one of the prophets of old. But one would still have been able to
say[42] that he had seduced and misled a 'small' people of illiterates
and ignoramuses and that his death on the cross had finally shown
his true identity, that of a blasphemer. It was thus the recourse to
the character types from the individual supplications that opened the
door of the biographical genre to the first Christian writers.

---

[42] And, as I have pointed out in *The Birth of the Gospels as Biographies*, this was
an accusation that was spread at the end of the first century.

CHAPTER IV

CHRISTOLOGY AND TYPOLOGY
IN THE NARRATIVE OF MATTHEW

The narrative of the Passion in Mark has shown how and why typology was able to provide a response to the scandal of a Messiah dying on a cross. In order to respond to the same difficulty, has the macro-narrative of Matthew proceeded similarly or has it used another model[1]?

Regarding the characterization of Jesus, if in Mark, typology is used extensively only in the Passion narrative, in Matthew it is dispersed throughout the macro-narrative; it is, of course, in his Passion narrative, which responds to the same challenge as in Mark, that of a final *anagnôrisis*, but it is present beginning with what is referred to as the Infancy Narrative (Mt 1–2) and continues with the help of different types – Moses, Jeremiah, etc. – throughout the ministry. The typological choices of the Matthean narrative are, as will be seen, decisive for understanding its purpose and status.

I. PSALMIC TYPOLOGY

Like the Passion narrative in Mark, the one in Matthew follows the model of the supplications of the persecuted just. In the

---

[1] In *The Birth of the Gospels as Biographies*, I have said why, when one takes into consideration the biographical question, the macro-narrative of Mark must be declared to be prior to those of Matthew and Luke.

tables that follow, each episode in Mt 26–27 takes up a motif from these supplications, from the plot and betrayal through the final cry. Like Mark's, the Matthean Passion narrative disqualifies all recognition/*anagnôrisis* by Jesus' coreligionists and only retains as pertinent that of God, who resurrects Jesus. But whereas in Mark, Pilate does not declare Jesus innocent – in Mk 15:14, he only asks about Jesus: "Why, what evil has he done?" –, in Matthew, without going so far as explicitly declaring Jesus innocent, unlike his wife (Mt 27:19), he dissociates himself from the will of the people who cry: "Let him be crucified", in a nevertheless astonishing statement, for it reverses the roles: "I am innocent (in Greek: *athôios*) of this man's blood!" Who is innocent, Pilate or Jesus? The modification of the Matthean narrative with the emphasis on Jesus' rejection by his own people invalidates neither the strength nor the impact of the psalmic model.

The Passion Narrative and Psalmic Typology

Anointing at Bethany

	Passages in Mt	**Passages in OT Psalms**
plot, told by the Nr	26:1-5	Ps 30/31:14; 63/64:5-7; 70/71:10-11
betrayal, told by the Nr	26:14-16	Ps 40/41:10

Jesus' Last Supper with the Disciples

	Passages in Mt	**Passages in OT Psalms**
announcement of the betrayal by Jesus	26:20-25	Ps 40/41:10
announcement of the disciples' flight and denial by Jesus	26:30-35	Ps 30/31:12/11; 87/88:19

Gethsemane
Jesus' Prayer

	Passages in Matthew	Passages in OT Psalms
prayer, said by Jesus	26:39-42	108/109:4
condition of Jesus's spirit, told by the Nr and by Jesus	26:37-38	41/42:6, 12; 42/43:5 54/55:3, 5; 37/38:11; 108/109:21/22
supplication, said by Jesus	26:39	88/89:27; 39/40:8
handing over to sinners, told by Jesus	26:45	139/140:5; 87/88:9

The Arrest

the disciples' weakness, told by Jesus	26:30-31	Zech 13:7
the disciples' abandonment, told by Nr	26:56	30/31:12/11; 87/88:19
Peter follows at a distance, denies, told by the Nr and by Peter	26:58, 69-75	37/38:12 the same adverbial expression, *apo makrothen* = at a distance

The Trial
Before the Sanhedrin

wanting his death, told by the Nr and members of the Sanhedrin	26:59, 66	36/37:22; 108/109:2; 30/31:14
false testimony, told by the Nr and the characters	26:60-61	34/35:11
Jesus' silence, told by the Nr and high priest	26:63	38/39:10
insults, told by the Nr and the opponents	26:67-68	68/69:8

Before Pilate

insults by the soldiers, told by the Nr and the soldiers	27:27-31	68/69:8

The Death on the Cross

drawing of lots for the clothing, told by the Nr	27:35	21/22:19
mocking of the adversaries, said by the passers-by	27:39, 41-44	43/44:15-16
gall/vinegar given to drink, told by the Nr	27:34	68/69:22
wagging their heads, told by the Nr	27:39	21/22:8
they tempt Jesus, told by the Nr and by the opponents	27:39-43	21/22:9; 70/71:11
Jesus' last cry, said by Jesus	27:46	21/22:2
soldier's gesture, told by the Nr	27:48	68/69:22

Jesus's Cry and the Soldiers' Confession

Jesus' final cry (Mt 27:46) and the soldiers' confession (Mt 27:54) are to be interpreted as in Mark. But the centurion, alone in Mark, is now found accompanied by all the subalterns charged with watching over the tombs in order to affirm: "Truly, this was a son of God!". The reasons for which these men make an act of *anagnôrisis* are different: it is no longer a matter of the way in which Jesus expired but of the apocalyptic signs orchestrated by his death; the latter is no longer only that of a persecuted just but the advent of the eschaton (Mt 27:54).

Up to Jesus' death, the Matthean narrator follows the model of the supplications of the persecuted just to highlight Jesus' rejection by his people, but what then happens is interpreted apocalyptically.

The Reasons for the Psalmic Model

The choice of the psalmic model for narrating the Passion could be surprising. Indeed, like Luke, Matthew additionally develops a prophetic typology, more precisely Jeremian, as we will see. Yet, the prophetic model combines recognition and rejection: the prophets are rejected and put to death before being recognized as such. If the Matthean narrator articulates the recognition, which rather dominates during the ministry in Galilee, and the rejection, which is pointed out beginning with the birth of Jesus (Mt 2) and is consummated during the Passion, he could not have been inspired by the narratives of the deaths of the prophets, for those that were in circulation were very short and did not correspond to the numerous episodes from the Passion of Jesus. But he had at his disposal Mark's, and from that, the model of the supplications, thanks to which was highlighted the absence of any *anagnôrisis* on the part of Jesus' coreligionists. We may affirm, without risk of error, that the psalmic model, where all are in league against the innocent, allowed the Matthean narrator to repeat a then well-known *topos* on the continual unruliness that led the Israelites to reject and put to death those sent by God. His narrative reports an absence of conversion and an even more serious rejection, since Jesus was the envoy par excellence, the Messiah of God.

Allusions to Jeremiah in the Passion Narrative

Even if the Matthean Passion narrative is largely inspired by the supplications of the persecuted just, it seems to echo other motifs from the Book of Jeremiah. In the first place, the wish to put to death the prophet (Jer 11:21)[2] in the form of threats are reminiscent

---

[2] Jer 11:21: "Therefore thus says the LORD concerning the men of Anathoth, who seek your life, and say, "Do not prophesy in the name of the LORD, or you will die by our hand". The Greek phrase *zèteô (tèn) psychèn*, "seek the life of", is perhaps taken from Jer 11:21 in Mt 2:19. See as well Jer 26:11.

of Jer 37/44:20; 38/45:15, 26. Secondly, a citation is very probable: Jer 26/33:15 repeated in Mt 27:4 and 27:25 that denotes a typological reprise[3]:

Jer 26/33:15	Mt 27:4 and 25
(if you put me to death, you will bring) **innocent blood** (*haima athôion*) (upon yourselves)	v. 4 Judas: "I have sinned in betraying **innocent blood**"
(you will have my) (innocent) **blood on you** (*eph'hymas*)	v. 25 the people: "His **blood be on us**"

In Mt 27:9-10, the narrator explicitly cites Jeremiah:

Then was fulfilled what had been spoken by the prophet Jeremiah, saying, "And they took the thirty pieces of silver, the price of him on whom a price had been set by some of the sons of Israel, and they gave them for the potter's field, as the Lord directed me."

This composite citation (Zech 11:12-13 and Jer 32:8-9) is attributed to Jeremiah because, according to commentators, he was at that time more well-known than Zechariah. If the rules followed by Matthew in order to combine these two passages are not the easiest to determine[4], this episode was clearly inserted at this point of his Passion narrative in order to make known that the characters of the narrative themselves recognize their responsibility, Judas explicitly and the chief priests implicitly. Indeed, if the first says openly to have betrayed innocent blood, the chief priests, by not leaving the thirty pieces of silver in the sanctuary, themselves recognize as well that it is blood money (Mt 27:6); but in saying this, they betray themselves (!) and implicitly admit to having corrupted Judas with

---

[3] As was said in ch. II, words common to the OT and NT passages do not suffice. The semantic parallelism must also exist, between Jeremiah and Jesus, between the opponents in Jer 26/33 and those in Mt 27.

[4] B. WITHERINGTON III, *Matthew*, coll. Smyth & Helwys Bible Commentary, Macon, Ga, 2006, p. 507, speaks of "exegetical gymnastics".

the silver[5]. As to the thirty pieces of silver, they are mentioned in order to point out, with the help of the oracle from Zech 11:12-13, that it is a derisory amount: "the lordly price at which I was paid off" said ironically by YHWH (v. 12)[6]. Thirty pieces of silver, the price paid to put Jesus to death.

How to interpret these echoes of the character Jeremiah? The reminders of Jesus' innocence and, in contrast, his opponents' responsibility clearly refer to Jeremiah's situation and lead us to say that, if the psalmic model prevails narratively, it is actually in the service of the prophetic typology. Not having a narrative of putting the prophets to death, the Matthean narrator adopted the Marcan model of supplications, but inserted into it allusions to Jeremiah, an innocent prophet, threatened with death, whose tradition said that he had been stoned, in order to imply that Jesus' death was that of a prophet. In order to be certain, this reading may be verified if, in the rest of the Matthean macro-narrative, there exist allusions to Jeremiah that progressively outline a typological relationship.

II. PROPHETIC TYPOLOGY

The Prophets in Matthew

The Matthean narrator uses more than the other Gospel narratives the substantive *prophet* and the verb *to prophesy*[7], in particular in what are called statements of fulfillment[8]. As to the typological

---

[5] WITHERINGTON III, *Matthew*, p. 507, refers to Deut 27:25: "'Cursed be he who takes a bribe to slay an innocent person.'" The statement is a fortiori valid for the author of the corruption.

[6] See also, Ex 21:32: "If the ox gores a slave, male or female, the owner shall give to their master thirty shekels of silver."

[7] Prophet (in Greek: *prophètès*) Mt 34x; Mk 6x; Lk 28x; Jn 14x; to prophesy (in Greek: *prophèteuô*) Mt 4x; Mk 2x; Lk 2x; Jn 1x.

[8] Mt 1:22; 2:5, 16, 17; 3:3; 4:14; 8:17; 21:4. Jesus uses the fulfilment formula twice, in Mt 12:17 (Is 42:1-4) and 13:35 (Ps 77/78:2).

interpretation concerning prophecy, it is stated by the narrator, by the crowds or by Jesus.

The Narrator

The Matthean narrator practically always leaves the typological statements to the characters of his narrative. The only time when he himself, as narrator, uses typology is found in Mt 3:4, where he implies, thanks to a scriptural echo[9], that John the Baptist is the antitype of Elijah[10], a reading later explicitly confirmed by Jesus: "and if you are willing to accept it, he [John the Baptist] is Elijah who is to come" (Mt 11:14).

The reader must not be surprised that the narrator so rarely uses, as narrator of course, prophetic typology in order to describe Jesus. As it is up to the narrative's characters to make pronouncements on Jesus, he leaves to them the responsibility of this identification and only refers to it in Mt 21:46: "[the chief priests and the Pharisees] tried to arrest him [Jesus], they feared the multitudes, because they held him to be a prophet".

John the Baptist and Jesus for the Crowds

Even the opponents of Jesus admit it (Mt 21:26, 46): for the crowds, John the Baptist and Jesus are prophets. When Jesus asks his disciples who people say that he is, the latter respond with a prophetic identification: Elijah, Jeremiah, one of the prophets (of old) (Mt 16:14). Beginning with the entrance into Jerusalem, the city in turmoil questions the crowds on the identity of the one whom they are acclaiming, and the latter explain themselves as they had previously done: "This is the prophet Jesus from Nazareth of Galilee" (Mt 21:11). At the end of his itinerant ministry, Jesus is thus well-recognized as a prophet by the whole of the population – the chief

---

[9] Mt 3:3: "For this is he who was spoken of by the prophet Isaiah when he said, 'The voice of one crying in the wilderness: Prepare the way of the Lord, make his paths straight.'" Cf. Is 40:3-4.

[10] Mt 3:4 that repeats Mk 1:6: "Now John wore a garment of camel's hair, and a leather girdle around his waist; and his food was locusts and wild honey". Cf. 2 Kings 1:18.

priests and the Pharisees being the exception – and this *anagnôrisis* is corrected neither by the narrator nor by Jesus, as we are now going to see.

Jesus and the Prophets

When Jesus speaks of the prophets and obliquely designates himself as one (Mt 13:53), it is in order to evoke his rejection and being put to death (Mt 5:12; 23:30, 34, 37)[11]. In Mt 12:39 he announces, still allusively, his own death that he gives as a (prophetic) sign by mentioning Jonah's stay in the belly of the sea monster[12], thus making himself the antitype of this prophet. Knowles also rightly sees in the Matthean version of the parable of the murderous wine tenants (Mt 21:33-44) another clue in favor of a Jeremian typology[13]. Indeed, in v. 35, the verb to stone (in Greek, *lithoboleô*), absent in the versions in Mark and Luke, probably is alluding to the *topos* of a stoning of Jeremiah, as testified to more or less during the same era in the *Lives of the Prophets* and the *Paralipomena of Jeremiah*[14]. The typological reprise is confirmed, in vv. 35 and 38 from the same parable, with the use of the word servants, in the plural (in Greek: *douloi*), in order to designate the prophets, which very probably is alluding to the expression "my/your servants the prophets" present more than fifteen times in the Old Testament, in particular twice in the Book of Jeremiah, with the same verb to send (in Greek: *apostellô*)[15].

The manner in which the Jesus of Matthew mentions the prophets is identical to that of the Jesus of Luke. The refrain is everywhere the same: in the past, the Israelites rejected and put to death the prophets that God sent to them; presently, they have done the

---

[11] It is a *topos* coming from Q, present as well in Luke: Mt 5:12 = Lk 6:23; Mt 23:29-32 – Lk 11.47-51; Mt 23:37 – Lk 13:34.

[12] Cf Jon 1:17: "And the LORD appointed a great fish to swallow up Jonah; and Jonah was in the belly of the fish three days and three nights."

[13] KNOWLES, *Jeremiah*, p. 111.

[14] *Lives of the Prophets*, 2:1; *Paralipomena of Jeremiah*, 9:19-32.

[15] God sends his servants the prophets: Jer 7:25; 25:4.

same to John the Baptist, a great prophet, Elijah of the end times, and will end by putting to death Jesus, the Son (Mt 21:38-39 and par.), himself also a prophet and despised by his own like all the prophets (Mt 13:57[16]).

The vocabulary of prophecy resurfaces during the Passion, but only once and from the mouth of the members of the high priest's entourage:

Mt 26:68	Mk 14:65	Lk 22:64
saying: "Prophesy to us, you Christ! Who is it that struck you?"	"And some began to spit on him ... saying to him, "Prophesy!" And the guards received him with blows	and asked him "Prophesy! Who is it that struck you?"

To the apostrophe: "Prophesy!" (in Greek: *prophèteuson* in all three versions) Matthew and Luke add: "Who is it that struck you?", implying that Jesus had his eyes blindfolded – the imperative used alone in Mark perhaps seemed to them incongruous – and consequently could not provide an answer. For the opponents who ridiculed him, Jesus became a powerless prophet, incapable of prophecy. The reader must, on the other hand, understand that he could no longer have any prophecies: Jesus' silence is that of the prophets put to death; he is for this reason a true prophet.

The connotation of the identification of Jesus as a prophet thus differs according to the speakers: during the ministry on the roads of Palestine, for the crowds it is positive and in the present, whereas for Jesus it is negative, principally oriented towards his rejection and his death to come.

The Prophet Jeremiah in Matthew

Knowles' monograph on Jeremiah in the Matthean work points out the current consensus of exegetes on the importance that

---

[16] The same idea in Lk 4:24.

this prophet has in Matthew. There are several reasons: during that era, he was considered as the prophet par excellence, his book was representative of all the prophetic books, he had announced the destruction of the Temple in Jerusalem and, above all, he had been harshly persecuted by the Jerusalemites of his day[17]. Additionally, Jeremiah is explicitly mentioned three times in Matthew[18], whereas there is nothing at all about him in the other Gospel narratives.

All the passages proper to Matthew and their parallels in Luke inventoried above show the importance of the prophetic theme in these two Gospels and confirm the presence of a Jeremian typology in several places of Matthew, a typology stated almost entirely by Jesus himself.

In his study, Knowles follows the Matthean narrative pericope after pericope in order to note all those where an allusion is made not only to the Book of Jeremiah but also to the person, as a type of Jesus[19]. Here retracing the route taken by this exegete is excluded, only recalling that the episodes preceding the Passion, where the Jeremian typology is present, allow showing that the latter is prolonged in the Passion narrative and, moreover, is structured by psalmic typology. In the list that follows, the typological relationship has been identified by taking into account the criteria proposed by Hays and Allison.

Before the Passion
- In Mt 21:13 "It is written, 'My house shall be called a house of prayer'; but you make it a den of robbers." Jesus' declaration to the sellers in the Temple, which is found as well in the other two Synoptics[20], is almost a

---

[17] KNOWLES, *Jeremiah*, pp. 81-95.

[18] The three times are in 2:17-18; 16:14 and 27:9. In 2:17-18 and 27:9 it is the book having this name and in 16:14 the crowds' typological identification of Jesus with Jeremiah.

[19] KNOWLES, *Jeremiah*, pp.162-222. M.F. WHITTERS, "Jesus in the Footsteps of Jeremiah", *CBQ* 68, 2006, pp. 229-247, has shown the importance of Jeremiah, a prophet of the Nations and the new covenant in Matthew. As he has little interest in typology, there is not space here to repeat his conclusions.

[20] Mk 11:17 = Lk 19:46.

word for word reprise of Jer 7:11: "Has this house, which is called by my name, become a den of robbers in your eyes?" Like Jeremiah, Jesus is criticizing his coreligionists' relationship to the Temple. And, like Jeremiah, it is for having stigmatized this attitude that he is going to be threatened with death (Jer 26:11).

The vocabulary and the semantic parallelism invite seeing here a typological allusion to Jeremiah established by Jesus himself.

- In Mt 21:35, in the parable called the murderous tenants, Jesus declares "the tenants [sent by the owner of the vineyard] took his servants and beat one, killed another, and *stoned* another".

As indicated above, the words "servants" and "stoned" invite seeing an allusion to the prophets and to Jeremiah in particular, the stoning of Jeremiah having by then become a *topos*. Once again, this typological allusion is attributed to Jesus.

- For Mt 23:37[21], "O Jerusalem, Jerusalem, killing the prophets and stoning those who are sent to you!", which is also a statement of Jesus, one can infer a typological allusion for the same reason as in Mt 21:35.

- Mt 23:38[22]: "Behold, your house is forsaken and desolate". Closely related to the verse that precedes it (Mt 23:37) in the Matthean macro-narrative, this statement of Jesus undoubtedly is alluding to several of Jeremiah's declarations (Jer 7:14; 12:7; 22:5; 26/33:9). Like Jeremiah, Jesus announces the fall of Jerusalem and the destruction of the Temple.

The typological allusion is valid because it is found in the same pericope as the verses previously noted and has the same characteristics.

- The same observation can be made for Mt 24:2 that announces the destruction of Jerusalem[23]: "Truly, I say to you, there will not be left here one stone upon another, that will not be thrown down".

During the Passion

The typological reading that underlies Jesus' declarations made before the Passion on the destruction of the Temple and Jerusalem invite seeing the same typology, prophetic and more precisely Jeremian, being extended throughout the Passion, with statements like those of Mt 27:4 and 24 confirming this reading[24].

---

[21] = Lk 13:34.

[22] = Lk 13:35. Cf. KNOWLES, *Jeremiah*, p. 185.

[23] = Mk 13:2. See Jer 7:14; 9:10; 26/33:9, 18 and KNOWLES, *Jeremiah*, p. 188.

[24] According to several commentators, Jesus' words over the cup in Mt 26:28 ("For this is my blood of the covenant, which is poured out for many for the forgiveness of sins") refer to Jer 31/38:31-34 because of the word *covenant*. One cannot, however, see in this verse a typological reprise, for a semantic parallel

The preceding observations invite concluding that the Matthean narrator takes up the Old Testament theme of the rejection and putting to death of the prophets[25] by giving it as much, if not more, dramatic intensity. But it is not only in order to point out a continuity, namely the rebelliousness of the Israelites and their rejection of those sent by God, but also in order to show, thanks to a *synkrisis* with Jeremiah, that Jesus himself is *really a prophet*, by the positions he takes on the Temple and Jerusalem as well as by his tragic fate[26].

Another conclusion stands out. The prophetic typology that runs throughout the Matthean macro-narrative is handled principally by Jesus, who emphasizes the rejection and putting to death of the prophets and thus announces his own death. This prophetic typology becomes more precisely Jeremian with Jesus' arrival in Jerusalem and is extended during the Passion, with Judas' confession before the high priests (Mt 27:4) and the people's response to Pilate (Mt 27:25). For the Matthean narrator, prophetic typology allowed resolving the question of the *anagnôrisis*, but in a manner different from Mark's, for the rejection was an integral, indeed obligatory, part, if one believes the *topos* then in vogue on the fate of the prophets.

III. MOSAIC TYPOLOGY

In recent decades, several studies have been published on the Mosaic typology of the first Gospel, some to minimize it, others to

---

between Jeremiah and Jesus does not exist. Indeed, if Jeremiah's blood was spilt, it was not for the forgiveness of the sins of all.

[25] As one knows, it is a Dtr theme.

[26] Cf. KNOWLES' observation, *Jeremiah* p. 161: "By depicting John, Jesus and the disciples as rejected prophets, and by comparing these both to one another and to the prophets of old, Matthew seeks to demonstrate that the fate of Jesus and those associated with him is consistent with that of all God's messengers".

highlight it. With Dale Allison's monograph, a complete and critical state of the question has at last been made[27]; his methodological
options allow determining with more certainty what could be typological in Matthew. From the Matthean narrative this author presents about twenty passages where, in the opinion of many, Mosaic
typology is at work[28]. Without repeating in detail his critical examination, it is possible to show that a Mosaic typology is present in
several Matthean pericopae, to determine its outlines and its reason
d'être. Not repeating the whole of the dossier is more than authorized as, for this author himself, all the passages do not have the same
degree of probability. Here are those where, in his opinion, the Mosaic typology is the most certain:

> The Moses typology, especially strong in the infancy narrative and the
> Sermon on the Mount, definitely shapes all of Matthew 1-7. It is also
> definitely present in the great thanksgiving of 11:25-30, in the narrative
> of the transfiguration (17:1-9), and in the concluding verses, 28:16-20.[29]

The Infancy Gospel Mt 1:16-2:23[30]

Beginning with the vocabulary, commentaries note that the citation from Hos 11:1 ("out of Egypt, I called my son") in Mt 2:15

---

[27] ALLISON, *The New Moses*, in particular the appendices on pp. 293-328.
[28] Mt 1:16-2:23 (Infancy Gospel); 4:1-11 (temptations in the desert); 5:1-2 (introduction to the Sermon on the Mount); 5:5, 8 (two beatitudes); 5:17-18 (the Law,
not abolished, but fulfilled); 7:13-27 (the end of the Sermon on the Mount); 7:28-
29 (the reactions to the Sermon); 8–9 (Jesus' miracles); 10 (the mission speech);
11:25-30 (Jesus' thanksgiving); 12:15-21 (Jesus and the Servant in Isaiah); 12:38
and 16:1 (what sign?); 14:13-21 and 15:29-39 (the two multiplications of the
loaves); 17:1-8 (the Transfiguration); 21:1-17 (the entrance into Jerusalem); Mt
23 (against the scribes and the Pharisees); Mt 24:3 (Jesus on the Mount of Olives
and his coming at the end of time); 26:17-31 (the Last Supper); 27:45-54 (Jesus'
death); 28:16-20 (the final directives to the disciples).
[29] ALLISON, *The New Moses*, p. 268.
[30] On the Mosaic typology in Mt 1–2, see the illuminating analyses of A. PAUL,
L'évangile de l'enfance selon saint Matthieu, Cerf, Paris, 1968, in particular pp.
153-161.

already explicitly refers to the time of the Exodus. They also point out the words and phrases from this book that are disseminated throughout Mt 1–2[31]:

Matthew	Exodus
1:18 before they (Mary and Joseph) came together (cohabited) (*prin è synelthein autous*)	1:19 before the midwife comes to them (the Israelite women) (*prin è eiselthein pros autas*)
2:13-14 for Herod is about to search (*zètein*) for the child, to destroy him (*tou apolesai auton*) (Joseph) departed (*anéchôrèsen*) to Egypt	2:15 he (Pharaoh) sought (*ezètei*) to kill (*anelein*) Moses 4:19 (Moses) departed (*anéchôrèsen*) to the land of Midian
2:15 until the death (*tès téleutès*) of Herod	2:23 the king of Egypt died (*etéleutèsen*)
2:13 take (*paralabé*) the child (*to paidion*) and his mother	4:20 So Moses took (*analabôn*) his wife and his sons (*ta paidia*)

But, as we pointed out in ch. II, vocabulary does not suffice. The semantic parallelisms are just as essential. Yet, the citation from Hos 11:1 in Mt 2:15 seems to relate Jesus and Israel – the word *son* designating the people in Hos 11:1 – and not Jesus and Moses. One could object as well that in Mt 2:13 Joseph must flee and take refuge in Egypt until the death of Herod, whereas in Ex 4:20 Moses, who had previously fled to Midian, can return to Egypt: the identical words are misleading, for they refer to opposite circumstances (before/after the death of the king) and to inverse journeys (out of Egypt or towards Egypt). To the first objection, Allison responds that along with the intertestamental Jewish tradition Matthew makes Moses, who emblematically represents the people, the son of God. To this argument based on the Jewish interpretation of the time, it is

---

[31] The table is ALLISON's, *The New Moses* pp. 155-156.

necessary to prefer that of the Matthean writing, for the narrator does not hesitate to remodel the narrative of the Exodus in his own way in order to describe the situation of the newborn Jesus. By itself, Hos 11:1 is concerned with the people of Israel, but placed as it is in Mt 2, it can only be valid for the Moses/Jesus parallel, for the surrounding verses do not speak of the people. Another objection also seems to undermine the typological reprise: if in Mt 2 it is foreigners who are going to worship the king of the Jews while his own people reject him, in the passages from Exodus called upon, it is a foreign king, Pharaoh, who threatens Moses. Certainly, but it is not Pharaoh's foreign origins that matter for Matthew, but rather his opposition to the will of God; Pharaoh and Herod thus have the same role, that of opponents. In spite of the differences, the semantic parallelisms, by far superior, established between Jesus and Moses make the typological reprise probable:

- Moses and Jesus, barely born, are threatened with death
- by the king of the region,
- but God assures their protection.
- He causes them to flee the threat;
- then, the king having died,
- He causes them to return to their people.

That in Mt 1–2 the narrator makes Moses the type of Jesus requires all the more acknowledging that Moses is the only great biblical character threatened with death at his birth. The question that is then raised is even more important: what is the purpose of the narrator's typological work in this Infancy Gospel? Let us not forget, Mt 1–2 is a biographical introduction in good and due form[32] that initiates the problem of the recognition of the royal or messianic identity of Jesus and of the rejection of which he will be the object. From his birth, the king/Messiah is *recognized and rejected* – recognized by foreigners and rejected by the highest political authority of his people, threat and death thus constituting, from the beginning,

---

[32] For a demonstration, see ALETTI, *Birth*, pp. 49-52.

the backdrop of the narrative. By pointing out the drama, the Matthean narrator makes his point of view known beginning with the introduction: if, from before his manifestation, Jesus was rejected and threatened, it is because he was not wanted; this rejection characterizes the way in which, according to a well-known tradition of the 1st century, Israel treated those whom God sent to her.

The Sermon on the Mount Mt 5–7

The Matthean formulas that frame the beginning and the end of the Sermon on the Mount take up those describing Moses ascending and descending the mountain:

	Moses	Jesus
to ascend the mountain (*anabainô + eis to oros*)	Ex 19:3; 24:12,13, 18; 34:1,4; Num 27:12., Deut 9:9; 10:1,3	Mt 5:1; 15:29
to descend the mountain (*katabainô + ek/apo tou orous*)	Ex 19:14; 32:1,15; 34:29; Num 20:28; Deut 9:15; 10:5	Mt 8:1

The closest parallels are those of Moses ascending in order to receive the tablets (Ex 24:12 and Mt 5:1) and descending with them (Ex 32:15 and Mt 8:1). The lexical correspondences not sufficing, it is necessary to review the semantic parallels that exist between Jesus and Moses, for to ascend and descend the mountain does not additionally imply that they have analogous roles.

What it is necessary to show is that Moses and Jesus both have a legislative role[33]. The difficulty comes from Jesus' at no time

---

[33] In Mt 5:1, it is said: He [Jesus] went up on the mountain, and when he sat down (in Greek verb *kathizô*), his disciples came to him". According to ALLISON, *The New Moses*, pp. 175-176, the seated position assuredly indicates the position of the teacher, as all accept, but it perhaps denotes a *topos*, that of Moses seated next to God, as PHILO reports it in *Sacrifices of Cain and Abel*, 8: "There are those who God causes to sit down (in Greek: *hidrusé*) next to him, such as Moses, to whom He says: 'Stand here (in Greek: *stèthi*) by me' (Deut 5:31)". Allison also invokes Deut 9:9 where the verb *wa'éshéb* would have the primary meaning "and

mentioning Moses in the Sermon on the Mount. Matthew could have had him say: "Moses said to you". Yet, he employs the passive – "You have heard that it was said (in Greek: *érréthè*) to the men of old/to you"[34] – that could be theological and thus have God as its subject. The *synkrisis* would then no longer be between Jesus and Moses but between Jesus and God, Jesus' directives being superior to those formerly decreed by God. It is understood that commentators have not gone in this direction, for the Jesus of Matthew does not claim to surpass God his Father. Allison is right to say that the "you have heard it said, but I say to you" does not signify on Jesus' part a rejection of what was previously prescribed – the Matthean Jesus does not declare the Torah obsolete, as his response to the young man who questions him indicates: "If you would enter life, keep the commandments" (Mt 19:17). The Torah is good and valid for all Israelites; the "more" is addressed to Jesus' disciples. This being said, for the Matthean narrator, the legislator of old is Moses, as attested to by the following:

Mt 8:4 – Jesus to the healed leper: "Go, show yourself to the priest and offer the gift that Moses commanded"
Mt 19:7 – the Pharisees to Jesus: "Why then did Moses command one to give a certificate of divorce?"
Mt 19:8 – Jesus' response: "Moses allowed you to divorce your wives"
Mt 22:24 – the Sadducees to Jesus: "Moses said, 'If a man dies, having no children, his brother must marry the widow'"

For Matthew, the rules of the Torah have thus been prescribed by Moses; the Sermon on the Mount thus truly established a

---

I sit down". Matthew also describes Jesus seated in a teaching position in 15:29 with the verb *kathèmai* that is also said of Moses in Ex 18:14, where Jethro says to his son-in-law Moses: "Why do you sit (*kathèmai*) alone, and all the people stand about you from morning till evening?" This is the position of a teacher and a judge. If such importance is given to the verb to sit down, it is obviously in order to provide a supplementary argument to the Jesus/Moses *synkrisis*.

[34] Mt 5:21 (on murder; Ex 20:13; Deut 5:17); 5:27 (on adultery; Ex 20:14; Deut 5:18); 5:31 (on divorce; Deut 24:1-4); 5:33 (on perjury; Lev 19:12); 5:38 (on the law of talion; Ex 21:24; Lev 24:20; Deut 19:21); 5:43 (on love of neighbor; Lev 19:18).

synkrisis between two legislators, Moses and Jesus, but also and especially between two stages of the legislation, the second taking the
prescriptions of the first to their extreme. We can return to the initial
question: if the "you have heard it said" is the equivalent of "Moses
said to you", why does Jesus not mention this person from the past,
the most illustrious of all! By not naming him, the Matthean Jesus
implies that the focus of the discourse is not on the inferiority of the
first legislator but on the relationship between the instructions, those
of Jesus being superior. In the Sermon on the Mount, the principal
typology is applied to the instructions, those of Moses being the type
of those of Jesus.

What then is the function of this typology? The following
section is going to allow responding.

The Charter of the Disciple Mt 28:16-20

The Function of the Matthean Narrative
The Matthean narrative ends with a discourse from the Resurrected One:

> All authority in heaven and on earth has been given to me. [19] Go therefore
> and make disciples of all nations, baptizing them in the name of the Father
> and of the Son and of the Holy Spirit, [20] teaching them to observe all that
> I have commanded you; and lo, I am with you always, to the close of the
> age.

The narrator does not close the episode by recounting what
the Resurrected One had become and by pointing out the Eleven's
reaction, what they could have said and then did. By not closing
Christ's discourse, he leaves the latter in the act of speaking, in order
to signify that the Resurrected One is still addressing the Eleven,
and through them, whomever listens to them in the present through
reading.

The composition of the declaration is interesting, for it indicates in the very space of the text that the sovereignty and the

presence of the Resurrected One (a) embraces and surrounds the mission of the Eleven (B):

a Jesus Resurrected, having all authority in the heavens and on earth

$$
B \begin{cases} \text{sends the Eleven on a mission:} \\ \text{goal = to make disciples} \\ \text{means = to baptize + to teach what he has prescribed to them} \end{cases}
$$

a Jesus Resurrected with them forever

Jesus begins by declaring (i) that he has full authority, (ii) that this authority is of divine origin, (iii) and of an unlimited extension since everything created is submissive to him, from celestial to earthly beings[35]. One sees why the declaration of his dominion precedes the sending on mission of the Eleven: it is by virtue of the power that has been conferred upon him that he sends them and assures them of his support. What is important here is the total and continual dominion of Christ, which determines that of the Eleven, the very content of their mission and the means by which it will be carried out. But if the duration of this efficient presence is specified, on the other hand, nothing is said of its modalities: will it be visible, invisible, will it be the equivalent of the gift of the Holy Spirit? This is not what the narrator retains, but the reality and the endurance of the presence, with its effects.

As to the disciples' mission (vv. 19-20a), it has no limits: all human beings, without any exception, are the addressees. The status is thus offered to all by the Resurrected One himself: the narrator is thus making it known that it is not a matter of a later apostolic decision, due to circumstances – the rejection of the Gospel by a

---

[35] The commentaries compare this ending with Dan 7:14 LXX: "And to him [the glorious Son of Man] was given dominion (Greek: *exousia*) and glory and kingdom, that all peoples, nations and languages should serve him; his dominion is an everlasting dominion, which shall not pass away, and his kingdom one that shall not be destroyed". Undoubtedly, but is it necessary to repeat that vocabulary alone does not suffice to determine the backdrop of Mt 28:16-20.

majority of Jews –, but that it comes from an order from the Resurrected One himself.

Thus, the Eleven disciples must in their turn make disciples. But disciples of whom? Of Jesus or of the Eleven and those who, following them, will go on mission? The verses preceding Mt 28:16 have signaled that the Eleven are themselves also disciples, and as for Jesus he does not say that the addressees of whom he is thinking will be disciples of the disciples: if all are disciples, they are those of the same Resurrected One. In fact, the rest of the sentence clearly indicates that these disciples will be his since the Eleven must teach what the Master has himself prescribed to them. The same sentence additionally delivers the function of the Matthean macro-narrative, for the reader, who has knowledge of all Jesus' discourses reported by Matthew, can no longer doubt, the Resurrected One confirms this to him, that in it is found and will always be found the charter of the being-disciple. Thus, the disciple's condition described in the Gospel is not the prerogative of only the historical companions of the earthly Jesus, but, on the contrary, it is the condition into which everyone is henceforth invited to enter. Everyone, that is those who are Jews and those who are not, from every culture and from every language.

The reader cannot but grasp the technique by which the Matthean narrative establishes the different statuses and apodictically states them, as wanted and established by the Resurrected One

- who is all powerful,
- whose word creates new relationships and new statuses,
- those of the disciple and of the book (Matthew) where the disciple will find his charter.

The ending of Matthew thus concludes with a final revelation, by the Resurrected One, of all the statuses: his, which is to be the master of all things; that of those who will evangelize – the authorized disciples, whose teaching is nothing other than the Master's; that of those who will be evangelized and will be disciples, like the first; lastly those from the book itself, like the apostolic testimony and faithful contents of Jesus' teaching, an always valid teaching, since the Resurrected One confirms its value for all ages: the commandments reported by Jesus' discourses and statements in Matthew thus remain the possession of the Church up to the close of the ages.

The passage's interest comes above all from the choice of the term 'disciple' (in Greek: *mathètès*) expressing our relationship to the Resurrected One. This term comes from the preoccupation of the narrator for whom Jesus does not leave his own deprived: thanks to the book, namely the Matthean narrative, *a charter for being-disciple*, they will know how to fulfill all justice, how to be perfect by the example of their master (Mt 10:24-25). Matthew must be the disciples' indispensable vade mecum. The Jesus of Mt 28:19-20a thus implicitly points out the necessity of the book: if the disciple wants to know what the Master expects of him, it is necessary for him to read Matthew's narrative, which is the charter of the Kingdom.

Jesus and Moses, the Narrative of Matthew and the Torah

Thus, we can return to the typology by which the Matthean narrator employs a double *synkrisis*, between Moses and Jesus and between the Mosaic Torah and his own book.
(a) Between Moses and Jesus, at the end of their respective journeys. Both

- ascend a mountain (Deut 32:49; 34:1; Mt 28:16),
- appoint the one/those who are going to succeed them, Joshua (Deut 31:7, 14) and the Eleven (Mt 28:18-20),
- so that they may tell their successors what they will have to do (Deut 31:23; Mt 28:19-20a),
- knowing that God, for Joshua, and Jesus, for the disciples, will be with them continually (Deut 31:23; Mt 28:20).

(b) Between the Mosaic Law and the book of Matthew.

Moses writes the book of the Law, and Jesus asks the disciples to transmit his precepts (Deut 30:10; 31:24; Mt 28:19). Both thus give an analogous function to the ordinances henceforth set out in a book, that of the Law for Moses and that of the life of Jesus for Matthew. As to Matthew's book, it has the same components as that of the Mosaic Law, since the instructions – the *halakah* – valid for ever, are wrapped up in the narrative texture, the *haggadah*. Consequently, the instructions in both are presented as a response of faith in and recognition of the powerful and faithful behavior of God (for the Mosaic Law) and of Jesus (for Matthew)[36].

What to conclude? For those who were expecting a teaching Messiah, having to interpret and explain the Torah to perfection, Matthew shows that Jesus more than responds to their hopes by interpreting and legislating in continuity with Moses. By describing Jesus as an antitype of Moses the legislator whose precepts he brings to perfection, Matthew thus takes into account Jesus' messianic identity and the recognition – the famous *anagnôrisis* – of this identity. If he presents the law-maker Messiah, Matthew also and especially gives to the Christian reader his narrative, a guide for the disciple that he must be.

Circumspectly, Allison analyzes other passages, shorter – among others the Transfiguration[37], the thanksgiving[38], and Jesus'

---

[36] For ALLISON, *The News Moses*, pp. 264-265, the background of Mt 28:16-20 is the same as that of the Testament of Moses, probably written in the 1st century of our era, which also relates the transmission of the powers between Moses on the point of death and Joshua. Matthew and the Testament of Moses would then be inspired by what had become a *topos*.

[37] The celestial voice asking the three disciples to listen to Jesus would be an allusion, according to several commentaries and studies, to Deut 18:15 "The LORD your God will raise up for you a prophet like me from among you, from your brethren – him you shall heed") and 18:18 ("I will raise up for them a prophet like you from among their brethren; and I will put my words in his mouth, and he shall speak to them all that I command him").

[38] Cf. Mt 11:29 ("for I am gentle (in Greek: *praüs*) and lowly in heart") and Num 12:3 ("[Moses] was very meek (*praüs*), more than all men that were on the face of the earth"), the only passage in the Greek Bible where one encounters this adjective. In Mt 11:29 an allusion to the Mosaic Law is possible as well, for if by the word 'yoke' (in Greek: *zygos*) Jesus is designating his instructions, the same metaphor is used by the Law ("The yoke of the Law") in the (Syriac) Apocalypse of Baruch (41:3). Could there have been a *topos* whose first witnesses could be

Last Supper – where the Mosaic typology is probably at work. An in-depth look is not necessary, for it would not change the overall results. The route undertaken up to here shows that a multiple figurative interpretation runs throughout the Matthean narrative: messianic in the introduction (Mt 2) and the Sermon on the Mount (Mt 5–7), prophetic during the peregrinations of Jesus (Mt 8–20) and psalmic during the Passion narrative (Mt 26–27), a disposition illustrated by the following table:

Typology	Mosaic	Prophetic	Psalmic
Jesus Messiah	Mt 2 by the Nr Mt 5–7 by Jesus		
Jesus Prophet		Mt 8–20 by the Nr, by the crowds, by Jesus and by the celestial voice Mt 27:4, 25 allusions to Jeremiah by the opponents	
Jesus Innocent Sufferer			Mt 26–27 by the Nr

IV. ROYAL TYPOLOGY[39]

The Royal Title

The messianic title "son of David", always used positively in order to designate Jesus, is more frequent in Matthew than in the

---

found in Sir 6:24-34 and 51:26 regarding Wisdom, which one knows to be identified with the Law in this book?

[39] The royal typology is more limited in its extension than the royal Christology. In other words, the royal theme in Matthew is not developed uniquely with the help of typology. On the royal theme in Mt 16:20 to 20:34, see C. BLUMENTHAL, "Vorbildhaftes Gottvertrauen: der matthäische Jesus zwischen tödlicher Ohnmacht und königlicher Macht", *Biblica* 99 (2018) 226-246.

other Gospel narratives[40]. Jesus is as well called king several times, with positive or negative denotations according to the speakers[41]:

Speakers	Positive Denotation	Ambiguous Denotation	Negative Denotation
the magi	Mt 2:2 (king of the Jews)		
citation from Zech 9:9 by the Nr	Mt 21:5		
Jesus	Mt 25:34-40 eschatological king/judge		
Pilate		Mt 27:11 (king of the Jews)	
Pilate's soldiers			Mt 27:29 (king of the Jews)
the writing on the cross		Mt 27:37 (king of the Jews)	
opponents at the foot of the cross			Mt 27:42 (king of Israel)

The reader will have certainly noted that the appellative "son of David" is used almost always by the characters who are addressing Jesus in order to obtain a healing and who recognize in him the Messiah, or even by the crowds who acclaim him at his entrance into Jerusalem, whereas "king of the Jews" or "king of Israel" is used during the Passion by foreigners or opponents. This being said, commentaries and studies are divided on the existence of a royal typology in Matthew. For some, it is present, and for others,

---

[40] Mt. 1:1 (by the Nr); 1:20 (said of Joseph *and not of Jesus*, by the divine voice); 9:27 (by the blind); 12:23 (by the crowds); 15:22 (by the Canaanite woman); 20:30-31 (by the blind outside Jericho = Mk 10:47-48; Lk 20:41); 21:15 (by the crowd at the entrance to Jerusalem); 22:41-45 (by the Pharisees = Mk 12:35-37).
[41] Whereas Jesus' coreligionists say "king of Israel", the non-Jews say "king of the Jews".

absent[42], for, in order to describe Jesus, Matthew keeps nothing from David's life and behavior[43]. Is a royal typology truly excluded?

Jesus' Entrance into Jerusalem[44]

In fact, when the titles "son of David" or "king of Israel/the Jews" designate Jesus, they do not convey strong semantic parallels between Jesus and David, and one can reasonably ask if the reading of the Matthean narrator is typological. Jesus' entrance into Jerusalem (Mt 21:1-10), where the royal connotations are undoubtedly the most numerous, from the pen of the narrator but also from the voice of most of the characters, should be able to enlighten us on the subject.

The Matthean Version and Its Parallels

If in order to search out the typology at work in Mt 21, a detailed comparative analysis of the three Synoptics is superfluous; on the other hand, the possible allusions to the Old Testament, in particular the traits connoting kingship, are most useful[45].

> And when they drew near to Jerusalem and came to Bethphage, to the Mount of Olives, then Jesus sent two disciples, [2] saying to them, "Go into the village opposite you, and immediately you will find an ass tied, and a colt with her; untie them and bring them to me. [3] If any one says anything to you, you shall say, The Lord has need of them,' and he will send them immediately." [4] This took place to fulfil what was spoken by the prophet, saying, [5] **"Tell the daughter of Zion, Behold, your king is coming to you, humble, and mounted on an ass, and on a colt, the foal of an ass."**

---

[42] KNOWLES, *Jeremiah*, pp. 236-237.

[43] It is generally accepted that in Mt 12:42 (The queen of the South "came from the ends of the earth to hear the wisdom of Solomon, and behold, something greater than Solomon is here") Jesus is proceeding typologically, stating indirectly his kingship, as in Mt 12:41 ("something greater than Jonah is here") his being-prophet.

[44] On the typology at work in this pericope, see NIEUVIARTS, *L'entrée de Jésus à Jérusalem*, chs. 2 and 3.

[45] They are in bold.

6 The disciples went and did as Jesus had directed them; 7 they brought the ass and the colt, and put their garments on them, and he sat thereon. 8 Most of the crowd **spread their garments on the road**; and others cut **branches** from the trees and spread them on the road. 9 And the crowds that went before him and that followed him shouted, "**Hosanna** to the Son of David! **Blessed be he who comes in the name of the Lord! Hosanna** in the highest!" 10 And when he entered Jerusalem, all the city was stirred, saying, "Who is this?" 11 And the crowds said, "This is the prophet Jesus from Nazareth of Galilee."

(a) The most obvious allusion common to the three Synoptics is clearly to Ps 117/118:25-26, thanks to the words *hosanna*[46] and the formula: "Blessed (be) he who comes in the name of the Lord"[47]. By themselves, this acclamation and this blessing do not have a royal connotation, but their importance comes from their being an *anagnôrisis* in good and due form. Jesus is acclaimed and recognized. But of what recognition is it a question? The royal coloration comes from the immediate context:
- in Matthew, the citation in v. 5, where, in order to facilitate his reader's understanding, the narrator, with the help of Zech 9:9, points out that Jesus is king;
- in Mark, the verse that follows, where the crowds, by acclaiming Jesus, welcome the reign that is coming, that of David, in others words the Messiah's (eschatological) one. The collective recognition in Mark 11:9-10, metonymic[48], thus corresponds to and echoes Peter's in Mk 8:29.
- in Luke, "the king" is added in v. 38.
(b) The royal coloration of the acclamations allows inferring that the words "ass" and "colt" also themselves refer to a royal milieu, as several Old Testament passages testify to, in particular 1 Kings 11:39 and 41[49]. If

---

[46] The *hosanna* is a transliteration of the Hebrew (*hôshyᶜah n'a* = save!). Initially a request for salvation, the phrase later became an acclamation, as one sees in this pericope. On the evolution of the expression, see, E. LOHSE, "Hosianna", *Novum Testamentum* 6, 1963, pp. 113-119.

[47] I am translating according to the Greek order that can lead to confusion. It is not necessary to link the phrase "in the name of the Lord" to "the one who comes", but to "blessed", as other passages show: 2 Sam 6:18; 1 Chron 16:2; Ps 128/129:8.

[48] Reign (in Greek, *basileia*) for the king (in Greek, *basileus*).

[49] 1 Kings 1:33: David to Zadok, Nathan, and Benaiah: "cause Solomon my son to ride on my own mule"; 1:38 (the execution of David's order). Also, 2 Sam 16:2: Ziba to David: "The asses are for the king's household to ride on"; 2 Sam

the names change – mule, ass, donkey, colt –, they are all humble, peaceful equines, princely mounts; horses, on the other hand, are always or almost always mentioned in the Scriptures in the context of war, the powerful of this world counting on them in order to vanquish their enemies. Matthew is the only one to explain the link between the beast of burden and the humility of the king who rides it (Zech 9:9)[50].

(c) The three Synoptics point out that the crowds spread their garments on the road taken by Jesus. Is it necessary to see an allusion to 2 Kings 9:13and/or a gesture of submission then practiced at the enthronement of a king, to which 2 Kings 9 and the Synoptics are both referring? Whatever the answer may be, the connotation is undoubtedly royal.

(d) The mention of the branches (Mt 21:8; in Greek: *kladoi*) or leafy branches (Mk 11:8), omitted in Luke, probably is alluding to the Festival of Booths[51], and its interpretation is in no way obvious. The colt and the spread garments already suggesting a royal enthronement, the branches on the ground along with the garments seem to enrich this royal connotation eschatologically[52]. But one can as well think that the motivations of the crowds are nationalistic[53]. Whatever the crowds' intentions, the Festival of Booths being at that time probably linked to the purification of the Temple[54], it seems preferable to respond narratively and say that Matthew, like

---

13:29: after the murder of Amnon, "Then all the king's sons arose, and each mounted his mule and fled".

[50] The commentaries note that the first stich of the citation is actually taken from Is 62:11.

[51] Cf. Lev 23:40; Neh 8:13-18.

[52] The Festival of Booths/Tabernacles is not only a memorial of the Exodus; it has as well an eschatological goal (see Zech 14:16).

[53] See NIEUVIARTS, *L'entrée de Jésus*, p. 93: "Matthew, in his narrative, evokes the ritual of the festival [Sukkoth], and if the political-religious connotations of the nationalistic type are not explicitly apparent, these texts at least discretely suggest them. Jesus will thus be able to enter into the temple and there consecrate the liberation of this place and perhaps the people from the victory of the occupier. It is *that* liberator about whom the crowds have a presentiment and who is already causing to break out on his way the joy of Sukkoth and the jubilation of the new dedication with accents similar to those of Sukkoth. If such a reading has been authorized, the arrangement of Matthews' narrative will only make more incisive the rest of his narrative: the occupier that Jesus is defeating at his entrance into the temple are the leaders of the people, and the people cannot contain their jubilation". It is impossible to determine if the motivations of the crowds were those.

[54] Cf. 1 Mac 13:51-52; 2 Mac 10:6-8.

Mark, knew how to use to his advantage the crowds' gesture in order to prepare obliquely for the following episode, that of the purification of the Temple.

(e) Matthew, Mark and Luke all mention that it is from the top of the Mount of Olives that Jesus sends his disciples to look for a colt. By itself, the information is neutral, but the royal context to the eschatological connotation invites seeing in it a redundant trait. By using Strack-Billerbeck[55], it has even been said that "at the time of Jesus one was persuaded that the Messiah would appear on the Mount of Olives"[56]. I have found nothing like this in this work. On the other hand, the sentence can actually be repeating Zech 14:5, which announces the coming on the Mount of Olives "of the Lord with his Saints" (*èxei kyrios* [Hebrew = YHWH] *ho theos mou kai pantes hoi hagioi met'autou*). Yet, as one knows, this eschatological royal coming of YHWH is attributed to Christ in the New Testament, and this, beginning with the Pauline letters (1 Thess 3:13; 2 Thess 1:7), but also in the Gospels (Mt 16:27). The link between the glorious coming of the Christ and the Mount of Olives is thus probable. Another element reinforces the probability of this reading: in these chapters of Matthew, several allusions are made to the book of the prophet Zechariah: in addition to Zech 9:9 in Mt 21:5; Zech 12:10 and 14 in Mt 24:30 (the coming in glory of the Christ at the end of time), Zech 14:5 in Mt 25:31 (another mention of the coming in glory of the Christ), lastly Zech 11:12 in Mt 26:15.

Through the features that they include – the Mount of Olives, the garments spread on the ground –, the three narrators also invite their respective readers to recognize in Jesus the Davidic and messianic king. But this interpretation is not their invention, for it relies upon the actual recognition of the crowds, a character in the

---

[55] STRACK-BILLERBECK, *Kommentar zum Neuen Testament aus Talmud und Midrasch*, C.H. Beck, Munich, 1926, vol. I, pp. 841-842.

[56] R. BARTNICKI, "Il carattere messianico delle pericope di Marco e Matteo sull'ingresso di Gesù in Gerusalemme (Mc 11:1-10; Mt 21,1-9)" *Rivista Biblica* 25, 1977, p. 7.

narrative. Matthew's originality is to have recourse to Zech 9:9 in order to explain this messianic reading[57].

The reading of the narrators and the crowds is actually created or engendered by Jesus himself: it is he who instigates the royal and messianic connotation. He indeed takes the initiative by requesting that one brings him (the ass and) the colt, and he sits upon it, indirectly inviting those who accompany him to recognize his royal identity. The reader will have undoubtedly noted that the citation from Zech 9:9 interrupts the narrative thread – Jesus' order and its execution by his disciples – and would have been better placed after v. 7, when Jesus seated about the ass and colt (!), descends towards Jerusalem. By citing Zechariah right after Jesus' order, the narrator implies that if Jesus asks that a beast of burden be brought to him, it is because he has Zechariah's oracle in mind.

The convergence of interpretations – those of Jesus, of the crowds and of the narrators – and the redundancy of royal allusions allow responding to the question concerning the presence of a royal typology in Mt 21:1-10. Of course, Matthew repeats nothing of the liturgical gesture of the enthronement of kings – the anointing with oil – nor of David's behavior, essentially military and warlike. Nevertheless, the reader who recalls how Mark, and Matthew with him, takes up and accumulates the traits of the supplications of the persecuted just in order to describe the way in which Jesus lived his Passion, cannot but see that the technique is the same in this episode of the entrance into Jerusalem, where the Synoptics have been able to construct their typological reading by repeating some of the concrete and significant traits of the royal enthronement that exist in 1–2 Kings. Like that of the Passion narrative, the typology is not fixed on a great personage from the biblical past; it only raises the traits that allow initiating a theme that is going to be followed in a

---

[57] The commentaries recall that the rabbinic literature read together Zech 9:9 and Gen 49:11. The first witness collected by STRACK-BILLERBECK, *Kommentar zum Neuen Testament*, vol. I, pp. 842-843 (Sach 9,9 in der rabbinischen Literatur', pp. 842-844) dated from 150 A.D.

paradoxical manner during the subsequent episodes, that of Jesus' royal and messianic identity.

The Royal and Messianic Typology in Matthew

Several difficulties in Mt 21:1-10 cannot be mentioned, for they would lead us too far from our subject. There is one, on the other hand, at the end of the pericope, that we cannot let pass in silence. When Jesus enters the city, which was in turmoil (literally: "shaken") and asked: "Who is this?" What do the crowds respond: "This is the *prophet* Jesus from Nazareth of Galilee."? Why do they not say: "It is the *king* Jesus" or it is the Messiah, Jesus of Nazareth"? Would they not have recognized the messianic royalty of Jesus? But the very fact that they spread their garments on his route indicates the contrary. Why then did they not announce to the Jerusalemites that he is king/Messiah? To say to the Jerusalemites, whose low esteem for the Galileans is known, that Jesus was from Nazareth would not have assured a frankly positive reception. But as the narrator points out no reaction on the part of the Jerusalemites, this means that the information was not made in order to be accepted or rejected, but that it is actually destined for the reader, who must only retain the title 'prophet'. On this same point, it is difficult to know what was the intention of the crowds, for the narrator does not reveal it. It is thus the intention of the latter that we must question. The title *prophet* is preferable to that of *king*, for (i) not being a Jerusalemite himself, Jesus could appear as a usurping *outsider*, (ii) it implies that the messianism of Jesus is not of a political and military nature, (iii) Jesus is truly a prophet and is going to undergo the fate of the prophets. After the recognition, there will be the rejection: would the episode of the entrance into Jerusalem thus be announcing this indirectly? That the end of the pericope is alluding to Jesus' future fate is implied by an implicit reprise of the city's prior reaction in Mt 2:3. As it was troubled by the question of the magi announcing the birth of a king, Jerusalem is similarly now in turmoil when Jesus enters, acclaimed by the crowds that accompany him. In short, if vv. 10-11 do not mention the immediate rejection, they hold it in reserve for the end of the macro-narrative. The episode of the entrance into Jerusalem has thus a twofold function: it brings to an end the process of the *anagnôrisis* – Jesus being recognized and acclaimed at the end of his itinerant ministry –, but it also sets in motion the question of Jesus' kingship, here recognized by the crowds, before then being mocked and rejected.

V. CONCLUSIONS

At the end of these developments, it is possible to conclude that typology has a decisive role in the Gospel of Matthew. Let us recall the reasons:

(1) The Passion narrative in Matthew has shown why and how the *psalmic* typology has provided a response to the scandal of a Messiah dying on the cross. By suggesting, like Mark, that, during his Passion, Jesus had the traits of the persecuted just, the Matthean narrator was able to show that the absence of an *anagnôrisis* discredited neither his protagonist nor his own narrative. But if for Mark, the psalmic model allowed eliminating all horizontal *anagnôrisis* – that of the people but also the disciples' –, for Matthew the same model allows showing that the people could go no further in its rejection of the ways of God.

As has been shown above, if the Matthean narrator followed the same model as Mark in order to recount the Passion of Jesus, it is because there did not exist in the Scriptures and in the intertestamental Jewish writings a narrative of the death of the prophets that was close enough or detailed enough.

(2) The *prophetic* typology, in particular Jeremian, has itself allowed verifying that, far from being counterproductive, the death of Jesus was a part of the required itinerary of the prophet. In general, it is after having been put to death that the prophets were recognized. Like the prophets, Jesus died rejected and put to death before being glorified by God and celebrated by more and more believers. The prophetic typology has thus allowed the Matthean narrator to show

that, far from being opposed to each other, the recognition and the rejection went hand in hand.

(3) The *Mosaic* typology has as well provided the Matthean narrator with the occasion (i) for describing Jesus as the antitype of Moses the legislator whose precepts he brings to perfection, thus taking into account his messianic identity, but also (ii) for making the writing that records his instructions the disciple's charter.

(4) With the *royal* typology, Matthew begins and ends his narrative in order to show that, if Jesus was not recognized as king/Messiah, it is because of the chronic disobedience of his people.

Is there a need to recall that, for points (1) and (2), Matthew has not proceeded typologically in order to establish a progression going from the old to the new, from shadow to reality, but rather in order to resolve two fundamental difficulties, that of an unrecognized Jesus – the absence of an *anagnôrisis* – and that of a Messiah dying on a cross – the Messiah of the Scriptures and the Jewish intertestamental literature essentially having a glorious character. One will perhaps object that this is not the case with the Mosaic typology according to which Jesus is manifestly superior to Moses, and the prescriptions of the Torah, although not eliminated, are taken to their perfection. We will return to this question over the course of the last chapter.

CHAPTER V

TYPOLOGY IN THE LUCAN NARRATIVE

In *The Birth of the Gospels as Biographies*, Lucan typology has already been the subject of a quite new and substantial presentation[1]. This chapter will repeat the thoughts that were made in that work on the reasons, means and goals of the third Gospel's typology, by providing other examples and showing why this narrative was neither able to nor ought to have proceeded like the other two Synoptics.

In the preceding studies, it has been shown:

(1) that in the Infancy Gospel (Lk 1–2), prophetic typology is already present, that its principal speaker is the narrator and that its presence is discrete, for the narrator never explicitly says when he is paralleling his characters with those of the Old Testament;

(2) that beginning with the episode in Nazareth (Lk 4:16-30), the typology, principally prophetic, is taken over by Jesus himself;

(3) that prophetic typology allowed the Lucan narrator to show that the final rejection of which Jesus was the object is in no way counterproductive, for it was the fate of the prophets, who were themselves also persecuted and, for a good number of them, put to death by their coreligionists.

---

[1] J.-N. ALETTI, *Birth*, pp. 89-106. See as well by the same author the *Cahier Évangile* 186, on the Lucan typology, published in September, 2018. I had already put forward a first series of theses on the typology of this Gospel in *Le Jésus de Luc*, published by Mame/Desclée in 2010 (out of print).

In order to establish that Jesus was a prophet, Luke thus had to find in Israel's Scriptures prophets with whom to parallel Jesus, for, as was said in ch. II, a parallelism is valid only because of the quality of the analogous semantic traits that exist between the type and the antitype. In *The Birth of the Gospels as Biographies*, the way in which the Lucan narrator establishes these semantic parallels was presented for the episodes of the widow of Nain (Lk 7:11-17) and the ten lepers (Lk 17:11-19). These pericopae being found only in the third Gospel, it was quite easy to highlight the way in which the narrator proceeds typologically. It remains to show with the help of a simple example that, even in the episodes that are common to Matthew and Mark, the Lucan narrator alludes to the prophets from the past more often than the other two Synoptics.

I. THE PROPHETIC LUCAN TYPOLOGY
   AN INITIAL APPROACH

The episode of the healing of an epileptic child is found in the three Synoptics in a sequence that is practically the same:

	Mt	**Mk**	**Lk**
Peter's confession	16:13-20	8:27-30	9:18-20
first announcement of the	16:21-23	8:31-33	9:21-22
Passion	16:24-28	8:34-38;	9:23-27
conditions for following	17:1-13	9:1	9:28-36
Jesus	17:14-21	9:2-13	9:37-43a
Transfiguration	17:22-23	9:14-29	9:43b-45
healing of the epileptic	17:24-27	9:30-32	
child	18:1-5		9:46-48
second announcement of		9:33-37	
the Passion			
the tax			
Who is the greatest?			

Clearly, Matthew and Luke follow the order in Mark, and the respective content of the pericopae is more or less the same, as the healing of the epileptic child shows. In Luke 9,37-43a, the identical or synonymous elements that the three narratives have in common are in boldface:

> On the next day, when they had come down from the mountain, a great **crowd** met him. [38] And behold, **a man** from the crowd cried, "**Teacher**, I beg you to look upon **my son**, for he is my only child; [39] and behold, a **spirit** seizes him, and he suddenly cries out; it convulses him till he foams, and shatters him, and will hardly leave him. [40] And I begged **your disciples** to cast it out, but **they could not**." [41] Jesus answered, "O **faithless** and perverse **generation, how long am I to be with you and bear with you? Bring** your son here." But Jesus **rebuked** the unclean spirit, and **healed** the boy, and gave him back to his father. [43a] And all were astonished at the majesty of God.

The common elements are the characters – the crowd, the father, the son, Jesus, the disciples[2] - and the actions – the father addressing Jesus, the report of the disciples' inability to heal, Jesus' reaction, initially negative but finally followed by the healing. The three gospel writers mention as well the twofold complication that sets in motion the plot and causes it to rebound, namely the illness, in other words the defect and the disciples' inability to eliminate it.

Unlike the Matthean and Markan pericopae (Mt 17:19-20; Mk 9:28-29) that end with a teaching on the reasons for the disciples' failure, that of Luke is the only one that can be qualified as a miracle narrative: to the request for a miracle, Jesus gives a positive response; the narrative quite briefly narrates the passage from illness to healing. The Lucan pericope additionally has several elements that are proper to it and recall the healing of Jairus's daughter (Lk 8:40-56):

1) the crowd that welcomes Jesus (8:40; 9:37)
2) a character from the crowd makes a request (8:41; 9:38)
3) concerning his only daughter/son
     (in Greek, *monogénès*; 8:42a; 9:38)

---

[2] But the unclean spirit is mentioned only in Mark/Luke, Matthew having chosen a Greek verb (*selaniázetai*; literally, to be moonstruck) that does not designate a character.

4) the reaction of those present
(amazement in 8:56; astonishment in 9:43a).

The semantic parallels – the father, the only son, Jesus who heals, the reactions of those present – that exist in both passages invite seeing a phenomenon of intratextuality.

A final element is found only in the Lucan pericope: the sentence "and Jesus gave him back to his father", which is reminiscent of Lk 7:15:

Lk 7:15: "and he gave him (in Greek, *edôken*) to his mother"
Lk 9:42: "and gave him back (in Greek, *apédôken*) to his father".

Yet, in Lk 7:11-17, it is also said that the widow's son was *an only child* (*monogénès*, 7:12). The parallel relationships that exist between the characters are as well such that it is again difficult to doubt the phenomenon of intratextuality that one finds, moreover, quite a few times in the Lucan macro-narrative. In the episode at Nain, as in that of the epileptic, there exist some common lexical elements: "crowd", "only son", "he gave him (back) to", and the final praise. To the criterion of the vocabulary is added that of the sematic parallels, as we just noted. But, as has already been shown[3], Lk 7:11-17 is as well referring to 1 Kings 17:17-24:

1 Kings 17:17-24	Lk 7:11-17
the widow (v. 20)	a widow (v. 12)
her dead son (vv. 17, 20)	a dead only son (v. 12)
the child cried (v. 22)	the dead man began to speak (v. 15)
[Elijah] delivered him	[Jesus] gave him
to his mother (v.23)	to his mother (v. 15)
you are a man of God (v. 24)	a great prophet has arisen (v. 16)

There are, nevertheless, differences between Lk 9:37-43 and Lk 7:11-17: the woman is a widow, but nothing is known of the man

---

[3] ID., *Birth*, pp. 97-98.

in Lk 9, except that he is a father; the first asks nothing of Jesus, whereas the second cries out in addressing him; lastly, the widow's son is dead, whereas the other child is not. But the verbal reprises and the parallel relationships – two only sons whom Jesus is going to return, alive and healed, to each parent – outweigh the differences, for they highlight both the gravity of the respective situations – to lose an only son – and Jesus' gesture that restores the familial relationships and results in these two parents receiving from his hand their child as a gift.

Therefore, what to conclude? Lk 9:37-43, being semantically parallel to Lk 7:11-17, and this episode, being in its turn semantically parallel to 1 Kings 17:17-24, the episode of the healing of the epileptic must, like Lk 7:11-17, be read typologically: in these passages, Jesus has Elijah as a type or prefiguration.

Given the typological coloration in Lk 9:37-43, another motif, namely the disciples' inability to heal the epileptic child, can be read in the same way. This motif is not a creation of the Lucan narrator; it comes from Mark, and being given this episode's Old Testament coloration, the Lucan narrator clearly has not eliminated it. The disciples' inability indeed recalls that in 2 Kings 4:29-31 where, the only son of the Shunammite woman being dead, Elisha, before setting out, sends his servant Gehazi to extend his staff over the child and return him to life. And the narrator adds: "Gehazi went on ahead and laid the staff upon the face of the child, but there was no sound or sign of life. Therefore, he returned to meet him, and told him, 'The child has not awaked.'" (2 Kings 4:31). To the semantic parallels that already exist – between the father and the mother, the only sons, Jesus and Elisha – this motif adds another, between the disciples and Gehazi. But, will one say, if Lk 9:40 is alluding to 2 Kings 4:29-31, has not the Lucan typology become incoherent? Is it indeed possible that, in the same pericope, Jesus has two different types, Elijah – 1 Kings 17:17-24 being the first episode to which Luke alludes – and Elisha – if there is an allusion to 2 Kings 4:18-37? The episode at Nazareth (Lk 4:16-30), where Jesus appeals to Elijah and Elisha in order to describe his own choices, allows dismissing any clumsiness and incoherence in Lk 9:37-43, the narrator only extending the typology constructed by his protagonist.

From the reading of Lk 9:37-43, let us retain for now that the prophetic typology of Elijah and Elisha is actually more present in the third Gospel than in the other two Synoptics. The Lucan typology is principally prophetic, and, in a decisive manner, it permeates the Lucan narrative material. This is what I am proposing to show by beginning with the beginning!

II. THE TYPOLOGY IN LUKE 1–2

The question of the beginning is of the greatest interest. Beginning with Lk 4:14, Jesus is not only the narrative's protagonist, he is also the one who is an omniscient character, who foresees events, interprets them authoritatively and shows their profound coherence: the other characters and the reader learn from his mouth the 'how' of the ways of God. If the discourse of Jesus at Nazareth in Lk 4 determines at that point the remainder of the third Gospel, the function of the preceding episodes is to present the origins (in Greek, the *génos*) of Jesus and John the Baptist, as this had to be done in the lives (in Greek, *bioi*), according to the Greek canons. But to this origin and to the Christology that it implies are added the techniques of an author and the status of the narrative itself.

The Parallelisms Between Characters

In Lk 1:5-4:13, Luke takes up a narrative process, well-known at that time, of the parallelism between two or several characters: between Zechariah and Mary, between John the Baptist and Jesus, between Simeon and Anna ... May it suffice to present the elements noted by all the commentators:

John		Jesus	Parallel Traits
1:5-7	//	1:26-27	presentation of the parents
1:8-11	//	1:28	appearance of an angel

1:12	//	1:29	trouble of Zechariah and Mary
1:13-17	//	1:30-33	discourse of the angel about the child
1:18	//	1:34	questions of Zechariah and Mary
1:19-20	//	1:35-37	angel's response
1:24-25	//	1:38, 39-55	reactions of Elizabeth and Mary
1:57	//	2:1-7	time of birth
1:58	//	2:8-20	the entourage hears, praises and rejoices
1:65-66	//	2:17-18	reaction of fear/astonishment
1:59-64	//	2:21	circumcision
1:67-79	//	2:22-38	human interpretations and prophecies
1:80a	//	2:40, 52	growth of the child
1:80b	//	2:39, 51	place of living – desert/Nazareth

The John/Jesus parallel goes as far as Lk 4:13, or even 4:15, that is to before the episode at Nazareth (4:16-30), which clearly begins a new stage in Jesus' life:

John		Jesus	Parallel Pericopae
3:1-6	//	3:21-38	presentation of John and of Jesus
3:7-17	//	4:1-13	their respective missions
3:18-20	//	4:14-15	summaries: end/beginning of their respective missions

Some of the parallelisms could be refined. What is important, for our purpose, is to grasp their meaning. Exegetes have shown that they aim to reveal the resemblances but also and especially the differences between the two infants, between their respective parents, as to their identities and their roles, their reactions and their fates.

The parallelisms, however, explain neither the narrative's beginning nor all its mechanisms. If John the Baptist is the precursor of Jesus, it is normal for the announcement of his birth to be recounted before Jesus'. What is less so, is how the narrator, who after the episode at Nazareth remains rather discrete, proceeds in order to depict his characters and reveal their profound identity. Who is it – the narrator's voice or a character in the narrative – that indicates to the reader that John is the Elijah of the end times, that Jesus is the Messiah, the Savior, the Son of God?

The Announcement to Zechariah

The Passage's Composition

The narrative division corresponds to the different scenes: according to the places, the characters' appearances and disappearances, the dialogue between the characters and the third person narration:

a   vv. 5-7 presentation of Zechariah and Elizabeth; childless;
            Elizabeth barren
b   vv. 8-10 service; entrance into the sanctuary; people outside
C   vv. 11-20 appearance and message of the angel Gabriel
b' vv. 21-23 people with expectations; Zechariah's exit, end of the service
a' vv. 24-25 conception of a child and Elizabeth's reaction: more shame

The scenes that correspond to each other are preceded by the same letter: in *a*, Elizabeth is barren, and in a', she is going to have a child; in *b*, Zechariah enters into the sanctuary, and in *b'*, he leaves it. One will have noted that the elements in vv. 8-10 are repeated in inverse order in vv. 21-23. As to the central scene, the longest, where the angel Gabriel and Zechariah are alone, it has its own composition, as we are now going to see.

The Appearance of the Angel and Its Literary Model (vv. 11-20)

These verses – similar to those of the announcement to Mary – owe their composition to that of passages from the Old Testament. The stages of the encounter are those of some of the angelic apparitions and announcements that occur in the Scriptures (for ex., Gen 17:1-21; 18:1-15; Judg 13:2-23): (a) apparition of an angel of the Lord, (b) reaction of fear or perplexity, (c) the word of comfort and (d) the message from the angel, (e) objection on the part of the recipient(s), (f) confirmation of the message, (g) by means of a sign:

Lk 1:11-20 John	Lk 1:26-80 Jesus	Motifs Repeated from the OT
(a) v. 11	v. 28	appearance of a divine messenger
(b) v. 12	v. 29	troubled reaction
(c) v.13	v. 30	word of comfort from the messenger
(ad) vv. 13-17	vv. 31-33	message concerning the child
v. 13	v. 31	his conception and name
vv. 14-17	vv. 32-33	description of his mission
(e) v.18	v. 34	question asked of the messenger
(f) v. 19	v. 35	messenger's response
(g) v. 20	vv. 36-37	sign provided by the messenger

From One Beginning to Another

The narrator begins the narrative with a few essential traits for getting to know Zechariah and Elizabeth: their origins, their life as faithful Jews, the absence of posterity and its cause, their age (vv. 5-7). The description is, however, slightly odd even if the reader can recognize a certain logic:

- the origin of the actors (a link with the past),
- their exemplary religious and moral behavior (present),
- the absence of heirs (failure: no future).

Why, after having emphasized the extreme religious fidelity of Zechariah and Elizabeth, does the narrative return to basely material traits: the absence of children and age? The narrator remains silent on the reasons for his choice. He thus is discretely inviting us to ask why, for, as numerous biblical texts attest, whoever remains faithful to the Law receives the divine blessings – numerous descendants, long life, honor and respect[4]. From the first episode of the Lucan narrative, it is thus necessary to return to the biblical universe, with its values, its promises – not always realized: Luke begins in a sort of backwards way. If the two elderly people remain irreproachable, why have they not received the promised blessing? Has the Lord forgotten them; does He even keep His promises? And the reader immediately discovers that the narrative aims to respond

---

[4] Cf. Ps 127/128; Deut 28:1-14; etc.

to these questions. If the angel comes, it is precisely in order to eliminate the deficiency pointed out by the narrator: Zechariah and Elizabeth will have a child, and their desire – that we know from Gabriel and not from Luke – is going to be realized far beyond what they could have hoped.

By saying that the beginning of the Lucan narrative leads us backwards, we could not find a more precise formula, for it is on the beginning of Israel's history that the narrator invites meditating. The unfolding of the narrative and the vocabulary evoke the situation of Abraham and the divine intervention that put an end to Sarah's barrenness. Most of the words chosen refer to the Book of Genesis and only the last parallel does not belong to the Abraham cycle: it is the cry of Rachel, herself also barren, at the birth of Joseph (Gen 30:23):

Lk 1:5-25	Genesis
narrator: blameless (v. 6)	17:1
narrator: advanced in age (v. 7)	18:11
narrator: barren (v. 7)	11:30
angel: do not be afraid (v. 13)	15:1
angel: your wife (v. 13)	17:19
angel: a son for you (v. 13)	17:19
angel: and you shall call his name (v. 13)	17:19
Zechariah: How shall I know this? (v. 18)	15:8
Elizabeth: to take away my reproach (v. 25)	30:23

In order to describe the prophetic role of John the Baptist, in vv. 15-17, the angel Gabriel as well repeats words from the Old Testament, Mal 2:6, in order to point out that he will have a mission of conversion, and more explicitly, Mal 3:1 and 3:23-24 (LXX), in order to describe him as the Elijah of the end times. We are going to return to this typological reading.

Luke thus begins by recalling the biblical past and invites his reader to do the same. But the narrator's memory returns to the very beginning of the promises, when everything happened thanks to a word that had to be believed. An inaugural word that Lk 1:5-25 repeats in its own way, for it is in recalling the first promise that it formulates another, also interwoven with biblical allusions: the future is being told with words from the past. What is the meaning of this reprise? Will nothing thus be changed? Does the narrator rather not invite recognizing a continuity, a coherence between the word from the beginning and that from the end?

Luke is here stating with discretion the rules of his narrative that will not end by referring to the biblical past at the very moment when he is describing the coming of the end. Thus, there is a constant to and fro where the coherence of a history and the narrative that recounts it is read.

The Enigma of vv. 18-20

The reader may come up against the interpretation that the angel makes of Zechariah's question in v. 20, even though the narrator puts on the priest's lips the same words as Abraham's (Gen 15:8), which have never been interpreted as a lack of faith. Just before the patriarch's question in Gen 15:8, the narrator indeed said that he believed in the divine promise (Gen 15:6). But it is precisely this reprise that must inform the reader. From the mouth of the patriarch the question is easily understood since Sarah and he are the first very elderly persons to whom God makes the apparently insane promise to grant a son. Yet, by repeating word for word Abraham's question, Zechariah shows that he knows the Scriptures. And if he knows the Scriptures, he must know that the divine promise will be realized: but then his question no longer has a raison d'être! One could not have narratively better expressed the contradictory situation in which Zechariah finds himself.

That the angel interprets his question as a sign of doubt, let us admit, moreover, without any discussion: the angel is God's envoy and his function makes him an omniscient actor! The difficulty rather comes from the narrative itself: if from the first episode, it is doubt, in other words the lack of faith – and on the part of a holy, blameless man – that constitutes the human response to the Good News, the remainder of the macro-narrative presages nothing good... But, as the subsequent episodes are going to show, lack of faith does not prevent the Good News from making its way: God realizes His plan of salvation in spite of Zechariah's doubt. For this reason, the episode becomes a prolepsis, an anticipation of the remainder of the Gospel. If the divine initiative encounters a lack of faith but is, nevertheless, able to put this at the disposal of its own omnipotence, it is because nothing will stop salvation. This resistance from the beginning allows predicting that of others, at the same time that it announces the victory of the God who remembers.

John the Baptist and Prophetic Typology

Let us recall how the angel Gabriel describes the future Baptist in vv. 15-17:

Lk 1:15-17	Old Testament
"he shall drink no wine nor strong drink" (v. 15)	Num 6:3-4
	Judg 13:14
"he will turn many of the sons of Israel to the Lord their God" (v.16)	Mal 2:6
	Mal 3:1
"he will go before him [God] (v. 17)	Mal 3:23
"in the spirit and power of Elijah" (v. 17)	Mal 3:24
"to turn the hearts of the fathers to their children" (v. 17)	Mal 3:1
"to make ready for the Lord a people prepared" (v. 17)	

The angel makes an announcement that is oriented towards its future fulfillment and is not in itself a reprise from the past. But he is describing John by referring to the power and spirit of Elijah and, in this way, is inviting Zechariah, and the reader with him, to recall the deeds of the prophet. From the mouth of the angel, Elijah is truly the type of John.

In Luke, the first typological interpretation does not have the narrator as speaker but the angel Gabriel, who is God's authorized spokesman. Thus, it is God who, through the voice of His angel, a character in the narrative, sets in motion the prophetic typology.

If the typological interpretation has for its first speaker the divine character Gabriel, who then are its addressees? Zechariah clearly, and with him, the reader. What follows truly shows that Zechariah had heard and understood the message, for in his canticle

– known under the name of the *Benedictus* –, he repeats the angel's words: "You, child, will be called the prophet of the Most High; for you will go before the Lord to prepare his ways" (Lk 1:76)[5]. The prophetic typology thus has for its second speaker another character from the narrative, Zechariah. That he characterizes his child as a prophet and that, like Malachi, he describes his ministry in relation to Israel point out that if the prophetic typology has God – through the voice of the angel – for the omniscient speaker, it is and must be recognized by the characters of the narrative, for it is first of all made for them, who must adhere to the ways of God. The problem of the *anagnôrisis* begins in a positive way, starting with the Infancy Gospel[6].

If Elijah is the type of John the Baptist, can he be Jesus'? We have seen, in ch. III, that in Mark, Elijah is the type of John the Baptist only. For Luke, on the other hand, he is the type of both, and in this there is no incoherence: Jesus himself, the authorized voice par excellence, is going to interpret his ministry in relation to Elijah (Lk 4:25); both being prophets, John and Jesus have for types the whole of the prophets, in particular the most famous, designated by the divine/angelic voice and by Jesus himself.

The reader will have ascertained this, without there being any incoherence or contradiction: in this pericope, Luke refers to several episodes from the Old Testament, to the announcements made to Abraham in the Book of Genesis but also to those in the Books of

---

[5] A reprise of Lk 1:17 that already cited Mal 3:1.

[6] To this problem of the *anagnôrisis* one must connect what is said about the insertion of psalms or canticles into the biblical narratives by S. WEITZMAN, *Song and Story in Biblical Narrative*. The History of a Literary Convention in Ancient Israel, Indiana University Press, Bloomington – Indianapolis, 1997. This author shows that the praises inserted into the biblical narrative aim to make normative the narrative that they are interpreting, as narrative in which is read God's action and plan for Israel and the world. Aware of God's salvific design, the narrative's actors welcome it, consent to it and confess it all as good news by their song, which repeats all the biblical history since the promises.

the Kings, where Elijah with strength and power presents himself as a unique witness of YHWH, the true God.

1 Samuel 1–3, the Biblical Background of Luke 1–2

Lk 1–2 and 1 Sam 1–2

Luke does not follow the writers of his time only with biographical conventions; the imitation goes as far as vocabulary and style, which is quite rightly qualified as anthological.

Throughout the episodes, the narration indeed repeats the words, expressions, stylistic turns and schemas of the Greek Bible. For a long time, it has been shown that for Lk 1–2 their author is largely inspired by 1 Sam 1–3. Here and there the situations and the characters' reactions are analogous; the borrowings are thus not only lexical or stylistic:

1 Samuel	Luke	Elements in Common
1:1-20	1:5-25	barrenness, prayer, answer
2:1-11	1:46-56	canticle of Hannah/Mary and return home
2:18-21	2:22-35	presentation in the Temple,
		the elderly man who blesses the parents
		the return home
2:21, 26	2:40, 43, 52	growth and grace before God and men
		the protagonist remains in the Temple

In addition to these motifs that form the narrative cadre, there exist others, also from the Old Testament, which confirm the extent of the process of imitation:

Biblical Texts	Luke	Motifs Repeated by Luke
Gen 18:3; 1 Sam 1:18	Lk 1:28, 30	divine goodness and grace to the recipient
Ex 8:12; Judg 6:12.16	Lk 1:28	"the Lord is with you" (+ laudatory name)
Judg 6:23	Lk 1:13;	"do not be afraid"
Gen 17:19	1:30	the child's name given by God (or His angel)
Gen 18:13-14	Lk 1:13, 31	gel)
Gen 29:32; 1 Sam 1:31	Lk 1:37	"with God nothing will be impossible"
		"the Lord has regarded the low estate of his
Gen 30:13	Lk 1:48	handmaiden"
		"all generations/women will call be blessed"

The imitation, as one sees, is at play on different levels – phrase, episode, action, macro-narrative:

Levels of the Narrative	Reprises from O.T. Passages
arrangement of the macro-narrative = genre and composition of each episode	1 Sam 1–3
the announcements =	Gen 17; 18; Ex 3; etc.
the praises/prophecies =	1 Sam 2: 1-10, etc
in each episode: words, phrases	motifs repeated from various books of the O.T.

The narrator's art is to have used the Old Testament passages without making an explicit citation – the one exception: Lk 2:23-24 –, to the point that it is difficult for whoever has little familiarity with the Old Testament to ascertain the many allusions. Over the decades, these numerous borrowings have led to there being doubt about the historicity of Lk 1–2. That the narrator has woven his episodes with the help of signifiers of diverse origin says nothing *a priori* on their historicity (or non-historicity). Rather it is important to see that if the narrator proceeded in this way, it is by virtue of his concept of the narrative, for he wanted the newness to be spoken of with words of old, and, reciprocally, for the promises from the biblical past to find their fulfillment in the interplay of the signifiers in Lk 1–2, where the announcement of what is going to happen – Gabriel's words are prophecy – is equally a discrete memory from past prophecies.

Jesus and Prophetic Typology
　　1 Sam 1–3 does not only serve the narrative cadre. In Lk 2:40 and 2:52, the narrator describes Jesus as 1 Sam 2:26 described young Samuel:

　　1 Sam 2:26: "Now the boy Samuel continued to grow both in stature and in favor with the LORD and with men."

Lk 2:52: "Jesus increased in wisdom and in stature, and in favor with God and man."

Does this mean that Jesus is himself also a prophet? In addition to the traits stated in Lk 2:40 and 2:52, are there others that allow giving a positive response to the question? It is important to note that the different narrative voices do not give the same traits to Jesus: if for the angel Gabriel, he is (explicitly) Son of David and Son of God, the narrator prefers to give him (implicitly) prophetic traits. As we will see, these two readings are not in opposition to each other but rather are actually complementary. The first gives the primary identity of the protagonist Jesus, and the second responds to the difficulty raised by the death on the cross: if Jesus is actually the Messiah, how did he come to die in that way? The prophetic typology allows giving an answer: being a prophet, he was, like them, rejected and put to death.

Thus, before the episode at Nazareth, the prophetic typology applied to Jesus is already found in Lk 1–2, but it is not explicit, only allusive, and it is the work of the narrator:

Lk 1–2 repeats 1 Sam 1–2 (Hannah and Samuel are the types of Mary and Jesus);
Lk 2:40 and 2:52 allude to 1 Sam 2:26.

But, one might object, if the prophetic typology in Luke has the function of responding to the difficulty raised by the dramatic death of the protagonist, by making Samuel the type of the child Jesus, the narrator uses a prophet who, if one believes the Scriptures, was neither rejected nor put to death. Would this not be an incoherence? The response is twofold: (i) by interpreting the birth and childhood of Jesus with the help of Samuel, the Lucan narrator shows that Jesus is a prophet from his conception and thus he did not become one from the exterior or posteriorly; (ii) in order to show that since the beginning Jesus is a prophet, Luke had only at his disposal from the Scriptures Samuel's conception and childhood; he thus did not have to look elsewhere.

III. JESUS INAUGURATES HIS TYPOLOGICAL READING

Beginning with the episode in the synagogue at Nazareth (Lk 4:16-30), the prophetic typology becomes explicit and is expressed by Jesus himself. It runs throughout his ministry, which goes from Nazareth to Jerusalem.

The discourse in the synagogue at Nazareth is not the first made by Jesus in a synagogue; it is indeed said that before arriving in his village he had already taught elsewhere and everyone sang his praises (Lk 4:15). It is as a man enjoying a good reputation that he returns home. But up to this point the narrator has not informed the reader of the contents of this teaching. With the statements made in the synagogue at Nazareth, it is the first time that Jesus presents himself, says to whom he is sent and why. This is an important episode, for it allows seeing how, through the voice of Jesus, Luke is obliquely preparing for the developments of his Christology and the dimensions of his typology.

The Text from Isaiah and the Prophetic Typology

The Envoy of Isaiah

After being given the scroll, Jesus unrolls it and *finds* (Greek verb *heuriskô*) the passage from Is 61:1-2. The formulation is at the least strange. For if Jesus *has found* this passage, it is what he was looking for, whether because it was the one that it was necessary to read that Sabbath or because he himself wanted to read it and not another. Whatever the answer, Jesus read what he wanted those present in the synagogue to hear, the text from Isaiah, thanks to which he indirectly presents himself. One may in fact say that this pericope initiates what has, henceforth, come to be called the "indirect Christology" of Jesus.

The text cited is composed from two passages (Is 61:1-2 and 58:6b) that Jesus was clearly not able to read since in Isaiah they are separated from each other. These sentences are put next to each other thanks to a *gezerah shawah*, an ancient Jewish exegetical technique, that one finds elsewhere in the New Testament, which consists of commenting on two biblical passages having one or several words in common (here, *release* [RSV]; in Greek, *aphesis*). [As the text that Jesus is supposed to read does not exist as such, the collage comes from the narrator, who clearly knows what a *gezerah shawah* is.

To what biblical figure is v. 18a referring? The citation from Is 61:1-2 requires that it be a prophetic figure. But it is necessary to distinguish between what is said for the inhabitants of Nazareth present in the synagogue and what the reader must understand. For the narrative's characters, the prophetic figure stands out, to the extent that not having heard the statements from the angel Gabriel to Mary nor those of the angels in Bethlehem to the shepherds, they do not know that Jesus is the expected Messiah. By mentioning Elijah and Elisha, in vv. 24-27, Jesus himself is taking up the prophetic tradition of Elijah and Elisha. On the other hand, the reader, who has in mind the angels' declarations in Nazareth and Bethlehem and who, with Jesus, heard the celestial voice at the Baptism (Lk 3:22), can as well think of the royal messianic filiation because of the presence of the verb "to anoint" in Lk 4:18, which translates the Greek *chriô*, from which comes the adjective *christos*, Christ, and because of the vocabulary of deliverance (in Greek, *aphesis*), which is reminiscent of the obliquely messianic formulations in the canticle of Zechariah (cf. Lk 1:71, 74 and 77). If the reader were to separate Lk 4:18 from the preceding angelic or divine declarations, he would be ignoring the Lucan technique of accumulation. In short, for the reader, the denotation is twofold, prophetic messianic but also royal.

But who are the poor to whom the prophet is sent to bring the Good News?

Who Are the Poor to Whom Jesus Is Sent?

Jesus says to the inhabitants of Nazareth: "Today this scripture has been fulfilled in your hearing" (v. 21b) and verses 22-23 clearly point out that all those present react as if they were the addressees of the message, the poor, the captive, the blind and the oppressed to whom Jesus is sent. In fact, it is Jesus himself who makes them the beneficiaries of the Good News, for his statement means that the relationships described by the prophet are being realized at the moment when he is addressing them:

Is 61	the Spirit	on me	to announce	to the poor
Today	(the Spirit)	(on Jesus)	(speaking)	to your ears

Verse 23 shows that Jesus has really understood that his compatriots expect that he has come to heal their sick: if he has returned to his village, is it not in order to perform miracles there as elsewhere? Yet, in the verses that follow, he seems to exclude them as beneficiaries of his salvific message. By indirectly presenting himself as a prophet, he is pointing out to them that, because a prophet, he could not be accepted in his homeland (v. 24). Almost all Bibles translate this sentence as if it were an observation, in others words a fact, in the present indicative: "no prophet is welcomed – or does not find welcome – in his homeland". The Greek adjective *dektos* is, however, a verbal adjective and means "receivable"; for this reason, it must be translated thus: "no prophet is receivable", in other words, "cannot be or could not be received", etc. But, will one say, far from rejecting Jesus, the Nazarenes are quite ready to accept him since they are astonished by the message of grace that comes from his mouth (v. 22). We will later see the reasons for which Luke chose this adjective and added a negation, which supposes a rejection, whereas nothing seemed to prepare for it. Let us only say here that by using this adjective in v. 24, the narrator is adeptly playing, in the homiletic manner of that time, with the *dektos* ("favorable") of the citation from v. 19 ("the favorable/acceptable year of the Lord"). The comparisons drawn from the Elijah and Elisha cycles in vv. 25-27 clearly indicate the reasons for which the prophet Jesus could not be received by his fellow citizens:

Like Elijah and Elisha, who were sent to some non-Israelites, Jesus is declaring to the Nazarenes that God has not sent him to heal their sick and thus can only provoke their jealousy. One must not then be surprised that in announcing their rejection Jesus immediately provokes it. His word thus becomes doubly prophetic, for it is by rejecting a certain image of the envoy and the expected signs on his part (v. 23) that Jesus gives the criteria that allows recognizing him as an authentic prophet: the announcement of his rejection (v. 24) and its quasi immediate implementation (vv. 28-29) confirm that what ought to have been a countersign (being rejected) is in fact what seals the truth of his having been sent. At the very moment when he is excluded and thrown out of the city by his fellow citizens, Jesus is a prophet and his word could not have more authority.

Jesus' attitude, one could object, all the same resembles a provocation, for the inhabitants of Nazareth were very well disposed towards him. Undoubtedly, his declaration can only offend his listeners. But preceding their rejection, Jesus as prophet is able to point out the orientation and the addressees of his mission. The purpose of the provocation is Christological: less than stigmatizing the rejection, it highlights Jesus' prophetic identity, as we will see later. Exegetes rightly emphasize the fact that the episode at Nazareth anticipates or prophesizes Jesus' rejection by the entire people. Undoubtedly the text is aiming at this – although it is necessary to question the extent of the rejection: all or only the religious authorities? – but the immediate verification of the sign announced must not be forgotten: it is one of the components that highlight the efficacy of Jesus' prophetic word, from the beginning of his ministry.

In short, from the beginning of his ministry, Jesus knows himself to be sent by God, he knows to whom he is sent, he knows in what his mission consists and accepts its conditions; and, in order to avoid all misunderstanding, he solemnly says it to all those who came to listen to him at Nazareth, thinking themselves to be the first beneficiaries of his message.

As for prophetic typology, it is clearly dominant in this episode. It is set in motion by Jesus himself who chooses the characters from the Old Testament, two prophets, of whom he obliquely declares himself to be the antitype. And from the prophetic typology, he principally retains the rejection and says so to his listeners, who are his coreligionists, those who cannot say that they have not heard.

Jesus and the Prophetic Tradition

Jesus' Oblique Christology

Actually, if Jesus does not designate himself as the prophet of the text from Isaiah, he also does not say to the Nazarenes that they are the poor, the oppressed and the blind of the same text nor, a little later, that they are going to reject him. All this is implied without ever being explicitly affirmed: it is by resorting to a saying, thus universal, that Jesus announces their rejection (v. 24); it is by drawing on the biblical past, far away in time and having different characters, that he points out his being sent to other cities (vv. 25-27). Since v. 23, Jesus' language is oblique because it implies one thing by another. So that others may recognize themselves in an oblique discourse, there must, of course, be sufficient clues, but the principle of such a mode of expression is to do whatever is needed so that others may understand even if their names are not used. The Nazarenes' aggressive reaction in Lk 4 shows that they have grasped what Jesus was saying to them.

The question raised by any oblique discourse is that of its raison d'être. As such, the metalepsis is linked to the recognition. Is it thus in Nazareth where Jesus will be truly recognized as prophet to the extent of the signs that accompany him (v. 23)? By not explicitly designating himself as the eschatological envoy, Jesus is going to have to leave it to the signs, in other words to the perspicacity of his fellow citizens. Yet he implies to them that they will not have signs, thus exposing himself to not being recognized by them. In fact, the oblique language allows for the recognition by avoiding the trap of a facile expectation too easily granted. Moreover, the recognition is going to be effected on two different levels of the discourse: 1) that of the reader, who is being asked to perceive in Jesus' rejection the paradoxical and authentic sign of his prophetic identity; 2) that of the Nazarenes, who sense that no sign will be granted to them and expel Jesus. If Jesus' listeners have grasped the relationships described by his discourse but not the theological and Christological significance of their rejection, the reader is invited to go further, to reread the Scriptures since the person of the prophet refers everyone to a past where there were prophets recognized or not by signs. In short, the reader is invited to compare and, in the end, to perceive a coherence, misunderstood by the listeners of Nazareth.

Jesus, Prophet

What is paradoxical in the announcement that Jesus makes of his (future) rejection is that it is formulated with the help of the past – and in the past (vv. 25-27). By saying that *no* prophet is acceptable in his own country, Jesus is not claiming to describe only the situation of the prophets of his time, in particular that of his predecessor John the Baptist. By using the present indicative 'is' (in Greek, *estin*) in v. 24, Jesus is referring, in the form of a saying, to the whole of the prophets from the biblical past taken as a unified totality: prophetic history's past enlightens the events at Nazareth and the whole of Jesus' itinerary.

The two examples chosen in vv. 25-27 are typical on a number of scores. First, because in the Books of the Kings and in the remainder of the Bible, the Elijah and Elisha cycles have an almost unequaled importance; there only and in a consistent manner in some of the narratives, prophetic activity is described that already assumes a rereading of Moses' thaumaturgical activity. Next, because the Jewish tradition itself retained Elijah as an eschatological figure (cf. already Sir 48:10-11), all prophetic history can thus be summarized in him: he refers to the model from the past, Moses, and he is the promise of the future time, a time of anger and salvation. But it is by following the third Gospel that one will see the profound reason for the choice of Elijah and Elisha.

That Lk 4:25-27 inaugurates the typology of Elijah and Elisha (applied to Jesus) in Luke is confirmed by a quick glance at the episodes that evoke the figure and the deeds of the two prophets[7]:

---

[7] The numbers in italics indicate the passages proper to Luke.

- Jesus in the desert 4:1-13 (cf. 1 Kings 19:1-8);
- the call of the disciples: *9:57-61* (cf. 1 Kings 19:19-21)
- the healings of lepers: 5:12-14; *17:11-19* (cf. 2 Kings 5);
- the healings of the blind: *7:21*; *14:13*; *14:21*; 18:35-43 (cf. 2 Kings 6:17, 20);
- the feeding miracles: 9:10-17 (cf. 1 Kings 17:7-16; 2 Kings 4:42-44);
- the resurrections of the dead: *7:11-17*; 8:40-56 (cf. 1 Kings 17:17-24; 2 Kings 4:18-37);
- the encounter with God on the mountain or the episode of the Transfiguration: 9:28-36 (cf. 1 Kings 19:9-18);
- the destroying fire: *9:54* (cf. 2 Kings 1:10-12);
- the Ascension: *Lk 24* and *Acts 1* (cf. 2 Kings 2:1-18).

In Lk 4:25-27, the two prophets are thus not simply fleeting illustrations: thanks to them, Jesus is proposing a reading of his entire ministry under the sign of continuity. He will give analogous signs and, in this way, will be able to be recognized as an authentic prophet. It is thus not only the rejection (v. 24) that makes Jesus a true prophet but also his salvific activity (and, consequently, the whole of the third Gospel), devoted to the same message, coming from the true God Himself: the absence of a sign at Nazareth is already a sign, but it does not suffice. There will be other signs. But which ones? And for whom? By mentioning Elijah and Elisha, Jesus immediately gives his template for reading, announcing with one stroke the genre and orientation of his prophetic activity.

Jesus thus has recourse to the Scriptures in order to show the coherence of the divine design at the very time of the rejection by his people and thus to give meaning to the present and future events of his prophetic ministry. At first glance, however, the choice that he uses is drastic and seems to distort the literary as well as the historic context. If vv. 25-26 summarize so well the difficult conditions of the deeds of Elijah, it is not the same for the following verse, for the beneficiaries of Elisha's thaumaturgical activity are not only foreigners, and, if the episode of Naaman in 2 Kings 5 is expressing a universalist message, one cannot find in it a polemic regarding any jealousy from the Israelites of that time. Are Jesus' affirmations thus not somewhat excessive? The commentators on Lk 4 have made an effort to show that Jesus' statements take up the reading that the Septuagint and even the apocryphal Jewish legends of the time made of the persecutions of which the prophets were the object. Let us only note here the importance of the references to Elijah and Elisha and through them to all the prophets for the remainder of the Gospel: the will for unification, manifest in Lk 4:25-27, is going to continue throughout the Lucan narrative (Lk 6:23; 11:47, 49-50; 13:33, 34). Beginning with Nazareth, Jesus thus sees prophetic history under the sign of universality and rejection, thereby charting a way through the Scriptures up to him, the prophet of the eschatological today. One can thus reverse the terms: if the Scriptures allow understanding the fate of Jesus, they, in fact, become a model and norm for Jesus' word that in this way acquires its maximal extension, since the prophetic history is found summarized in it, unified at the very moment when it is appealed to in order to clarify the present.

The Function of the Scriptures in Luke 4

Thus, in each of the two parts of the episode at Nazareth, the Scriptures hold a quantitively important place. The problem is determining their respective functions.

The passage from Isaiah has an (indirect) designative function, which is not the only one, for it engenders and defines the relationships of the narrative at Nazareth. The initial situation of need – there are the poor, oppressed, blind, and captive, which conditions the relationships in Is 61, is going to disappear: the poor are going to receive the Good News, the captive, deliverance and the blind, sight. The passage is also describing the conditions thanks to which this need is going to be able to be eliminated: (1) the choice of an Envoy of the Lord; (2) the gift of the means that allow him to complete his mission (the anointing, the presence of the Spirit); (3) the sending of the proclamation and the deliverance. But if in vv. 16c-20a the Scripture defines the relationships and thus opens a history of salvation, the fact remains that these relationships are still formal: to what events and thus to whom is the passage alluding? It is through the words of Jesus that the different roles can be assigned and that this Scripture finds its today (v. 21).

If Is 61:1-2 determines the new relationships prophetically, it says nothing of the modalities of the fulfilment of the prophet's mission, the conditions in which the envoy will accomplish his mission, nor especially how he will be recognized by his listeners. Thus, what is necessary is a template of reading, criteria that allow this recognition: this is the function, in the second part (vv. 23-27), of the recourse to the Elijah and Elisha cycles.

The complementarity of the two references to the Scriptures is clear. The text from Isaiah indeed allocates the roles and finds itself, by the word of Jesus, confirmed as a prophecy of the last events, but it says nothing of the whole of the history of salvation in its twists and turns and its great figures. As to the passage on Elijah and Elisha, it would only state a law of continuity and discernment concerning the recognition of the prophets but without a link to a possible culminating point in the series, if there had not been the text from Is 61 and its confirmation as eschatological prophecy.

But vv. 25-27 give some referents to the categories enumerated in v. 18. Who are the poor, the captive, the blind, if not those foreigners in search of the true God and who are the object of His mercy, those precisely about whom Jesus' interlocutors are not thinking? But, and it is the second piece of information provided by the paralleling of the scriptural texts, if it is Scripture that allows interpreting the Scriptures – there is nothing, moreover, that conforms more to the exegetical principles of the Jewish commentaries of the era –, it, nevertheless, does not do it without the fulfilment: between Is 61 and the details obtained thanks to 1 and 2 Kings there is the Jesus event. It is the eschatological today that allows pulling together both the whole of the Scriptures as prophecy, as a coherent unit oriented towards its end, and thus choosing the criteria of its interpretation, that is the biblical passages that will clarify the others. For our purpose, what is actually important is that Jesus himself

– *and not the narrator* – gives, in vv. 25-27, the rules for the interpretation of Is 61.

Another question, that of the addressees, is raised by the linking of the citations: if there is a clear correspondence between the poor, the captive, etc., in vv. 18-19 and the foreigners in vv. 25-27, does the remainder of the third Gospel not contradict this correspondence, to the extent that Jesus did not himself go to the pagans – one knows that unlike Mark and Matthew, Luke does not mention the journeys to Tyre, Sidon and Caesarea? Of course, but that is what actually makes this Gospel an open-ended narrative, at least at this level, with the second half of the diptych being the Book of Acts. In this sense, the prolepsis of Lk 4:25-27 is external since it does not find its realization within the third Gospel. But what it is indicating is capital: where thus could the early Church, and we who follow, have found the reasons for announcing the Gospel of mercy to sinners, Israelites and especially pagans, except in the authority of an extraordinary word, that of Jesus, alone capable of showing how such an announcement was in perfect continuity with the divine plan of salvation. Lk 4:16-30 has the function of presenting the founding act of this exegesis.

The Typological Exegesis of Jesus

By commenting on Is 61 with the help of 1 and 2 Kings and by thus showing their profound semantic correspondences, Jesus shows that he considers the Scriptures as a unity that finds its fulfilment in him. Noting the analogies is already recognizing in the Scriptures an internal coherence, and Jesus is not the first to have proceeded thus. But the relationship between the antitype and types involves more: it sees this unity oriented towards an end, the Christ. At Nazareth, Jesus inaugurates this exegesis since he proclaims as fulfilled the prophecies concerning the Good News of salvation and points out how the biblical history allows understanding this fulfilment, in other words how it had been prepared. What is important is that it is Jesus himself who is the first, and, in the first discourse reported by the Lucan narrator, he practices this typological reading: his word thus acquires a maximal extension. His word is indeed prophetic, in the sense that it determines the present and the future of the narrative's actors with regards to salvation. It is also in this way that it unifies the biblical past. In Lk 4:16-30, Jesus is really the prophet, the interpreter par excellence: of the Scriptures, of the past, of the present, of the future.

It is, however, important to note that at no time does Jesus' typological reading say that Jesus is superior to the prophets of whom he is the antitype. More than establishing a relationship of inferiority or superiority, his reading aims to promote a recognition: he is a prophet sent, like Isaiah, to announce deliverance, and like Elijah/Elisha, to the poor who are foreigners. In Lk 4, the typology has the function of establishing the roles thanks to which there will or will not be an *anagnôrisis*. But the recognition to which the typology invites is not and cannot be automatic, as the Nazarenes had experienced it. The listener, the contemporary of Jesus, but also the reader are unceasingly invited to a long back and forth between the Scriptures and the events of Jesus' public ministry, but especially between the Scriptures and the episodes of the Passion since it is precisely there that the concepts of coherence, unity, fulfilment seem to fail or dissolve. We will see that the inaugural lesson in Nazareth recalls that of the day after Easter (Lk 24). The connection to the designation (who is the anointed of the Lord?) is clearly not the same in the two chapters: in Lk 4, Jesus does not explicitly declare that he is the Christ, whereas after the resurrection, at the end of the journey, the designation will be able to be made explicit – for the disciples, for it is inseparable from faith. Nevertheless, if Lk 4:16-30 invites the reader to these long searches through the Scriptures for the events related by the Lucan narrative, why does one not find or finds so few – Lk 22:37 is the only exception –, in the chapters that follow this masterful lesson on exegesis, explicit citations similar to those of Matthew (before the Passion) or of John (during the Passion): "Thus was fulfilled what was announced by the prophet (or Scripture)..."? We will return to this.

The Question of the Recognition

Numerous narratologists have outlined their own taxonomy, diachronic or synchronic, of the narratives. Without repeating all their distinctions, let us only mention here that the Lucan narrative is not driven only by a plot resolution, in the sense that the reader would have to ask himself: what is going to happen? who is going to prevail? are they going to put Jesus to death, or will he succeed in escaping them?, etc. As to the characters, in particular Jesus, are they not in the service of such a plot? Rather it is the opposite that is true, since it is the events that have the function of making Jesus and his interlocutors truly and deeply known. The narrative that unfolds before our eyes is rather a plot of revelation where the process of the recognition of Jesus' prophetic identity is going to be set out: is he going to be recognized for who he is, by whom, when and by what signs? Will the recognitions be of the same degrees? To produce a narrative that aims for a recognition of Jesus entirely determined by a progressive revelation of this very Jesus thus seems to be the dominant characteristic of the Lucan text. But, will one ask, could the other Gospels not have been similarly defined? Do they not have the goal of revealing to us the identity and salvific function of Jesus, and is not the first artisan of this revelation Jesus himself, by his behavior and his speech? Yes, up to a certain point. But Luke alone inaugurated Jesus' ministry with an episode (Lk 4:16-30) where the principles that are going to innervate the remainder of his narrative are systematically presented and where the very word of Jesus engenders the remainder of the narrative.

Some Typological Difficulties

Elijah, A Type of John the Baptist or of Jesus?
In Lk 1:13-17 the angel describes John the Baptist with the traits of Elijah, and in Lk 4:25-27 Jesus describes his ministry as similar to that of Elijah. But if John the Baptist is truly the Elijah who announces the Messiah – for Gabriel being a celestial envoy

cannot be mistaken –, Jesus then cannot be this Elijah. Is the prophetic typology of Luke coherent?

Since it is the apodictic and divine words of the angel that say John the Baptist is the only one who is the Elijah of the end times, it thus cannot be doubted at all, and this is corroborated by Jesus himself in Lk 7:24-27: Going to be baptized by John, "What then did you go out to see? A prophet? Yes, I tell you, and more than a prophet. This is he of whom it is written: 'Behold, I send my messenger before thy face, who shall prepare thy way before thee.'" If Jesus declares that John is the one who prepares the way of the Messiah, he is implicitly accepting that he himself is not the Elijah of the end times. But the Lucan typology does not primarily consist in making the type and the antitype identical and thus in some way making the type valid only for a single character of the Gospel narrative but rather in bringing out the common traits that allow connecting Jesus to the prophetic line. More than the persecution and the rejection, the Lucan narrative provides evidence of the traits that Jesus had in common with Elijah and Elisha, among others, in the miracle narratives. By making Elijah the type or the prefiguration of John the Baptist and of Jesus, the Lucan narrator thus causes no clumsiness or incoherence at all.

Moses in Matthew 5–7 and Elijah in Luke 4

Unlike the first discourse in Matthew where Jesus is, in reference to Moses, a legislator and perfectly interprets the will of God (Mt 5–7), Luke presents him as a prophet similar to Elijah and Elisha. This difference is clearly attributed to the project of each Evangelist: if, for Matthew, Jesus is the one who promulgates the charter of the disciple and if this charter is written down in his book, one understands that he wanted to highlight this aspect from the beginning of Jesus' ministry. On the other hand, by proposing to show that Jesus is truly a prophet and perfectly fulfills the vocation and destiny of the prophets, Luke wanted to show that, from the beginning of his ministry, his protagonist was aware of being such and of having to go as far as the fate of the prophets. These differences thus come from each narrator's project. What is important for our purpose is to note that these differences are expressed typologically, which emphasizes the importance that typology had for the elaboration of the gospel narratives.

IV. PROHETIC TYPOLOGY DURING THE MINISTRY OF JESUS

In the episode at Nazareth, Jesus emphasizes the rejection of which the prophets are the object, and one must ask what are the reasons for his rubbing his listeners the wrong way, even though they were so desirous of listening to him and seeing him perform healings in their village. By saying that a prophet is not acceptable (in Greek, *dektos*) or cannot be accepted in his country, Jesus is repeating a commonplace that finds its confirmation in the Scriptures and that was transmitted up to the Jewish writings from around the Christian era, namely that the prophets had been persecuted by their fellow Israelites and many were even put to death.

Why is Jesus repeating this *topos* instead of moving towards the expectation of his listeners? It is clearly not a matter of a pronounced taste that he would have had for suffering, but, as has already been said, a key idea that is going serve as a guideline through the Lucan narrative.

In the developments that follow, one will see (1) that the use of typology is firmly linked to the question of the *anagnôrisis*, (2) that the typology of the Lucan narrative is principally prophetic, the reasons for which we will try to determine, (3) that this prophetic typology begun in Lk 1–2, in an implicit way by the narrator and that beginning in Lk 4 is taken over by Jesus, who states it and develops it in an explicit manner, is going to continue up to the end of his ministry (Lk 19).

Typology and Recognition

Before showing that in the Gospels typology has the function of responding to the question of the recognition (in Greek, *anagnôrisis*) of Jesus as the envoy and Messiah of God, let us recall that at that time one only wrote lives of illustrious men, known and recognized for their teaching and actions – military leaders, political men, philosophers and orators. The biography of an unknown, like Jesus of Nazareth, was unthinkable, *a fortiori* if he had been rejected by his contemporaries and remained so for the following generations.

The challenge of the first Christian generations was thus to write biographies of Jesus by showing that he had been recognized during his ministry, assiduously followed and acclaimed by the crowds. Some Gospel episodes end with the amazement or acclamation of those who are present at his miracles and hear his teaching. But the final recognition was missing: Jesus died alone, abandoned by his disciples, accused of blasphemy and put to death. How to interpret the contrast between the admiration of many during the itinerant ministry and the ignominious death, that of criminals? To the Christian group for whom his death was salvific, the representatives of Judaism of that time could object that, even if Jesus had succeeded in seducing the crowds, he had not been able to fool the religious elite of the country and additionally had been abandoned on the cross by God, whose messianic envoy he claimed to be.

The authors of the Gospels have met the challenge and succeeded in showing that the recognition of their protagonist Jesus had certainly taken place during his ministry in light of his miraculous actions, but they were as well able to propose a coherent reading of his Passion and his death that was capable of bringing about their readers' recognition. During the ministry of Jesus in Galilee and throughout the ascent to Jerusalem, the recognition of Jesus' prophetic identity by the crowds was possible thanks to the type of actions implemented, for they recalled those of the great prophetic figures of former times. It is this connecting of Jesus to biblical figures from the past that constitutes the major part of the typology of the New Testament narratives. The thoughts that follow are proposing to show that it is prophetic typology that best accounts for the Lucan narrative material.

Before seeing how the Lucan narrative elaborates its typology, it is important to provide some information about the voice in Luke that states the typological relationships. (1) Certain correspondences are made by the narrator in the form of allusions. Thus, the first episode in Luke, that of the announcement to Zechariah, is entirely typological, for it places the divine promise and Zechariah's response in line with the divine promise of numerous descendants and Abraham's corresponding response in Gen 15, but it is a matter of an allusion, not in any way an explicit referral. It is the same in Lk 7:15, where the narrative voice says that Jesus "gave the [living] child to his mother", like Elijah to the widow of Zarephath and with the same words as in 1 Kings 17:23 (in Greek, *edôken auton tè mètri autou*). These typological allusions are made by the narrator and have for their sole addressees the readers – those clearly having a sufficient knowledge of the biblical books (indeed biblical languages). (2) In other passages, as we will soon see, it is Jesus himself who states the typological relationships and does so for the benefit of the listeners of that day, the disciples and crowds who are listening to and following him.

To the two principal speakers, the narrator and Jesus, correspond two series of typological statements, respectively in Lk 1–3 and Lk 4–19. In other words, the typology of Luke is split between two groups, a first that precedes the episode of Jesus at Nazareth (Lk 4:16-30) and a second that takes its point of departure from there. Previously, it was a question of the typological reading made in Lk 1–2 and Lk 4:16-30; it remains to see how the typological reading made after the episode at Nazareth functions.

The Typology of Jesus after Luke 4 and Its Reasons

Jesus, A Prophet Recognized as Such

As we saw, Lk 4:24-27 initiates the typology of Elijah and Elisha that is applied to Jesus, a typology that is practically going to dominate up to Peter's confession. The list of the principal passages has already been made above[8]. It is important to note that in this first part of the ministry, the different characters of the narrative question the identity of Jesus and for the most part eventually say that he is a prophet: the prophetic theme is mentioned several times in these chapters and by different characters. For to be a prophet, it is necessary to be both recognized and rejected. Recognized by his words and his actions, like Moses, Elijah and Elisha, but also rejected by his contemporaries for denouncing their refusal to want to worship the one YHWH and to practice the justice wanted by Him. In short, these are the two essential components for being able to say that someone is truly a prophet.

If Elijah and Elisha are the principal figures used by Luke, the typology is not limited to them, for it is used to show that what is a stake is the recognition of Jesus' prophetic identity. And this problem is going to be developed in two complementary parts. In the first, it is the aspect of recognition that is going to be favored, for Jesus is going to be recognized by his countrymen as a prophet, and, in the second, it is the rejection that is going to constitute the principal leitmotif. Jesus' ministry can thus be divided into two parts that take up and develop the prophetic components presented in Lk 4. The first part goes *grosso modo* up to Peter's confession, and the second runs throughout the journey to Jerusalem, up to Lk 19:44, which can be diagramed in this way:

Jesus' Discourse at Nazareth Lk 4:20-30

admired and recognized and, immediately afterwards, rejected and threatened

Lk 4:22   Lk 4:28-29

Jesus, A Recognized Prophet = Lk 5:1 – 9:21   Jesus, A Prophet Rejected and Put to Death = Lk 9:22 – 19:44

That the recognition prevails in the first part of the ministry is amply proved by the accumulation of questions on Jesus' identity:

---

[8] Cf. p. 118-119.

Characters	Verses	Recognition of Jesus' Identity
the people	7:16	"a great **prophet**"
Jesus	7:19-22	describing John the Baptist in connection to him (a reprise of Is 61:1, the passage read in Lk 4:18-19)
Jesus	7:24-27	describing John the Baptist in connection to him as **prophet** + to prepare his ways
Simon	7:39	"If this man were a **prophet**..."
persons present at Simon's	7:49	"Who is this, who even forgives sins?"
the disciples	8:24-25	"Who is this whom the elements obey?"
the possessed man	8:28	"Jesus, Son of the Most High God"
the people	9:7-9	John the Baptist, Elijah, one of the old **prophets**
Herod	9:7-9	"Who is this?"
the people	9:18-20	"Elijah or one of the old **prophets**"
Peter	9:18-20	"The Christ of God"

One will certainly have noted that the disciples repeat to Jesus what the people were saying and what had gone as far as reaching Herod. It is beginning in Lk 7:16 that Jesus is declared a *prophet*, a declaration that the rumor mill is going to spread and amplify. One could not minimize the importance of this appellation: it means that those who approached Jesus, heard his teachings and saw his actions have perceived the continuity that existed between him and Israel's prophets, the most famous, Elijah, or the closest, John. Luke thus wants to make us understand that he has not invented the idea of the continuity decades later – at the time of the Church – in order to justify what no one was able to perceive during Jesus' ministry, but that he was already at that time recognized and accepted by most, even if they could go no further in the designation.

The characters' reactions are dispersed throughout the first chapters of the ministry and extend to all the population, from the humblest to the most elevated (Herod). Many follow Jesus in order to hear him or to be healed, and his identity leaves no one indifferent. That the recognition and the prophetic typology are strongly associated cannot be denied. An episode like Lk 7:11-16, proper to Luke, greatly emphasizes this, for it takes up Jesus' statement in Lk 4:25-26 and ideally summarizes this section of the Gospel that is carried by the question of the recognition of Jesus' identity.

Have the characters, who in Lk 7:16 declare "a great prophet has arisen among us", made the connection between Jesus' gesture and that of Elijah? The text does not say so, but this is not impossible, given the other miracles already performed by Jesus – a later passage (Lk 9:18) will indeed say that many saw in him the Elijah of the end times. For the reader, on the other hand, the recognition is facilitated by the verbal correspondences, in particular that of Lk 7:16 and 1 Kings 17:23 ("he gave him to his mother") but especially by Lk 4:26-27, where it was already a question of the widow of Zarephath. These are the signs which are devoted to recognizing the visit from God. But these analepses invite reading the context of the passage, which will allow giving to this episode more depth.

After the Sermon on the Plain, Jesus enters into Capernaum where he heals a slave on the point of death. A progression thus can be read from one episode to the other, for in 7:1-10, at Capernaum, Jesus heals *a dying man*, and in 7:11-17 at Nain, he brings back to life *a dead young man*, son of a widow. These two miracles are not isolated from what follows: in his response to the envoys from John, Jesus refers to the resurrections of the dead performed by him: "the dead are raised up" (7:22). The function of the episodes at Capernaum and Nain then appear clearer: the narrator is preparing for the question on Jesus' identity and the latter's response. Thanks to these two acts of power and the other healings – those that preceded and those that the narrator enumerates in the summary that follows in 7:21 –, Jesus will be able simply and implicitly to say: "See what I have done!" But the recognition is possible because these signs correspond to an expectation, itself sparked by a promise: in his response, Jesus echoes a text from Isaiah already read at the time of the episode at Nazareth and to others, mentioned above, once again indicating that it is necessary to see in all this the fulfilment of prophecies.

What it is necessary above all to retain for our subject is the relationship that exists between the episode of the widow of Nain and Jesus' statement at Nazareth on Elijah's envoy to the widow of Zarephath: this typological relationship reminds us that it is Jesus who, since the beginning of his ministry, has inaugurated the typology concerning him and that he himself has put it to work by his gestures and his words in Lk 7 and, from there, in the whole of the first part of the ministry.

Rejection and Prophetic Typology

Once the process of the recognition of the prophetic (for the crowds) and messianic (for the disciples) identity comes to an end with Peter's confession, Jesus begins the second section of the prophetic typology, henceforth negative. As the rejection is only going to take effect with the entrance into the Passion, it is a matter only of explicitly formulated announcements by Jesus – and by him alone.

If these announcements are not dispersed throughout the journey, they are, nevertheless, found in some passages so that those who heard Jesus, as well as the reader, may recall the importance of the *rejection* component, by which Jesus is recognized as a true prophet:

Announcements	Verses	Rejection, Sufferings, and Death
Jesus	9:22	1st announcement of the Passion
Jesus	9:43b-44	2nd announcement of the Passion
Jesus	11:29-32	"except the sign of **Jonah**"
Jesus	11:47	"you build the tombs of the **prophets**"
Jesus	11:48	"your fathers killed the **prophets**"
Jesus	11:50-51	"the blood of all the **prophets**"
Jesus	13:33-34	"Jerusalem, killing the **prophets**"
Jesus	17:17	"Where are the nine?"
Jesus	18:31-34	3rd announcement of the Passion

As Lk 7:11-16 was the representative episode of the *recognition* section in the first part of the ministry, Lk 17:11-19, itself also proper to the Lucan narrative, is representative of the second part, the *rejection* section. Commentators rightly emphasize the incongruity of the injunction of Jesus to the ten lepers ("Go and show yourselves to the priests"), for it assumes that these men are no longer leprous, whereas they still are – one went to see the priest not in order to be healed by him but in order to have him note the healing already effected and to ask him to celebrate the rite of purification (Lev 14). In short, by obeying and accepting an apparently crazy order, the ten lepers show their complete trust. It is thus hard to see why, at the end of the episode, Jesus seems to stigmatize the lack of faith of those who did not return "to give thanks" in his presence. He did not ask them to return, and they have quite certainly obeyed his order by going to show themselves to the priests. If the faith of the ten is not placed in doubt, it is the Christic coloration of the Samaritan's that points out the difference: the latter judged it more important to return to praise God at the feet of Jesus, without his ever having suggested it. By behaving in this way, the Samaritan points out that, for him, to praise God and "to give thanks" to Jesus are, henceforth, inseparable. There is thus a *plus*: if the ten have had total trust in the word of Jesus, the faith of the Samaritan is, henceforth, expressed christologically, in that it associates God and Jesus, through whom the salvation of God comes. It is this *plus* that Jesus highlights and on this *plus* that he questions his coreligionists, the Jews: will they be able or will they want to take the same step, to praise God in and through Jesus, to recognize in him their savior? By asking the crowds, who are present at the thanksgiving of the Samaritan, where the other nine healed lepers are, Jesus is implicitly raising the question of his identity and this to his own people: only a Samaritan, a man considered as a bastard and schismatic by the Israelites of the time, has understood that it was, henceforth, impossible for him to separate the praise of God from the thanksgiving to Jesus. For the subject that occupies us, Jesus' final question joins the announcements of rejection mentioned above: will his people recognize him? The negative response will be given during the Passion narrative and the death of Jesus.

As the theme of the recognition was above linked to the prophetic typology, that of the rejection and prophetic typology is here also going to go hand in hand. The drama described in this episode is that of the non-recognition, of the indifference or the rejection demonstrated by the people of Jesus. Let us recall that in addition to its typological nature, the episode of the ten lepers makes, with the same discretion, an allusion to the discourse at Nazareth, where Jesus declares to his countrymen: "And there were many lepers in Israel at the time of the prophet Elisha; and none of them were cleansed, but only Naaman the Syrian" (Lk 4:27). Thus is fulfilled Jesus' prophecy related to the type of ministry to which he knew himself to be called, at the same time that the composition of the Lucan diptych is designed so that the discourse at Nazareth announces the ministry of Jesus and is applied to the Passion of Paul in Acts 21-28. For the Gospel alone, let us point out only the episodes concerned with emblematically indicating the two components of the Lucan prophetic typology, recognition and rejection:

| 1 Kings 17 | Lk 4:25-26 | Lk 7:11-17 | recognition |
| 2 Kings 5 | Lk 4:27 | Lk 17:11-19 | non-recognition |

Let us lastly point out that the beauty and subtlety of Lk 17:11-19 comes from the way in which the Lucan narrator unites and articulates the two Christological components, royal and prophetic, that were only contiguous in Lk 4. The typology is that of Elisha – Elisha is the type of Jesus –, but by falling at his feet, the Samaritan at the same time initiates the royal theme that is progressively going to take over in what follows in the macro-narrative. Discretely, through the narrative's signifiers, Jesus becomes the point of convergence of the expectations and hopes of the past.

Henceforth, it is possible to describe how the Lucan narrator has proceeded in order to construct his typology, beginning with the episode at Nazareth. First, by concentration, by being focused on

Jesus' prophetic identity, then by accumulation, in other words by allusions or declarations repeated throughout Jesus' ministry. The following table repeats these elements by showing how the narrative has arranged the two components, positive and negative, of the prophetic typology as the key for reading Jesus' identity:

Jesus' Discourse at Nazareth Lk 4:20-30
Admired and Recognized Lk 4:22 and, immediately afterward, Rejected and Threatened Lk 4:28-29

Jesus, A Recognized Prophet = Lk 5:1 to 9:1	Jesus, A Prophet Rejected and Put to Death = Lk 9:22 to 19:44
7:16 the people: a great prophet 7:19-22 Jesus: v. 22 = Is 61:1 7:24-27 Jesus: JB + to prepare the way 7:49 the people: who is this who forgives sins? 8:24-25 the disciples: who is this the elements obey? 8:28 the possessed man: Jesus, Son of the Most High 9:7-9 Herod: who is this? 9:18-20 the people: Elijah, a great prophet 9:18-20 the disciples: the Christ of God	the announcements of the Passion by Jesus 9:22; 9:43b-44; 18:31-34 11:29-32 Jesus: an evil generation ... Jonah 11:47 Jesus: you built the tombs of the prophets 11:48 Jesus: your fathers killed the prophets 11:50-51 Jesus: the blood of the prophets 13:33-34 Jesus: Jerusalem who kills the prophets 17:17 Jesus: where are the other nine?
representative episode = Lk 17:11-19	representative episode = Lk 17:11-19

The Raison d'être of the Lucan Typology

One is, therefore, better able to see why the Lucan narrative developed a typology in two sections. The *recognition* component was indeed necessary; it was necessary that Jesus' identity be recognized by most of his coreligionists. But, as the elite had recognized in Jesus neither the prophet of the end times nor the Christ or Son of God, it was important to show that their refusal to believe in no way threatened the truth of Jesus' prophetic and messianic identity; thanks to its two sections, the Lucan typology will honor this necessity. Far from being counterproductive, Jesus' rejection and violent death shows, on the contrary, that he was truly a prophet, like his precursors put to death by his fellow Israelites. The Lucan typology is thus in the service of the problem of the recognition of Jesus' prophetic identity.

The Lucan narrator chose the prophetic typology in order to characterize Jesus because recognition and rejection are inseparable. Constituting an essential component of the prophetic identity, the rejection in no way threatens the truth of the prophetic (and messianic) identity of Jesus. The choice of the prophetic typology thus assures the continuity with the biblical past and shows *a contrario* that there is absolutely no separation between Jesus and the tradition which he gives as a reference.

V. THE TYPOLOGY OF THE END OF THE MACRO-NARRATIVE

We have up to now ascertained that it was by having recourse to prophetic typology that the Lucan narrative was able to respond to the challenge of a biography where the recognition of the protagonist's identity by the other characters of the narrative could not be missing. Prophetic typology indeed allowed providing a valid key for reading Jesus' ignominious death, by showing that this death was in no way counterproductive. But up to the entrance into Jerusalem, it was only a matter of statements; Jesus indeed repeats that a (true) prophet had to die (i) in Jerusalem, (ii) rejected and (iii) put to death, handed over by his own people.

Innocence and Recognition in Luke 22–23

Jesus' Death, The Death of a Prophet?
If several times Jesus announced that the death of the prophets would be his, in the Passion narrative, echoes of prophetic figures

are practically nonexistent. One only encounters a single explicit
appellation in the mouth of the guards who are ridiculing Jesus:
"Prophesy [Be a prophet]! Who is it that struck you?" (Lk 22:64).
This cannot be interpreted as an absence, for the narrator makes the
events of the Passion the effectuation of Jesus' statements on the
death of the prophets (cf. also Lk 22:37). The Lucan Passion narrative cannot be read apart from that which precedes it, announces it
and justifies it.

If one encounters the vocabulary of prophecy in the Lucan
Passion narrative only once, one must, however, ask if Lk 23 does
not indirectly allude to the accusation of false prophecy. In Lk 23:2
and 5, the religious leaders indeed say to Pilate that Jesus perverts
and stirs up the people – the Greek verb *apostrephô*, repeated by
Pilate in v. 14: "You brought me this man as one who was perverting
the people". If the accusation can be understood politically, for the
members of the Sanhedrin who formulate it, it is also implicitly religious: turning the people away from the ways of God by his teaching, Jesus would thus be a false prophet; it seems that the Jewish
accusation against Jesus as false prophet was already circulating at
the time of the gospel writers and notably of Luke. By emphasizing
the recognition of Jesus' innocence, both explicitly (by Pilate, the
judge, by the thief crucified with him, lastly by the centurion) and
implicitly (the women of Jerusalem, all of the crowd present at the
foot of the cross), the Lucan narrator thus makes the Passion and
death the proof thanks to which Jesus' prophetic identity finds its
ultimate confirmation.

The Necessary Recognition

Compared with the Passion narratives in Mark and Matthew,
where the psalmic model was used in order to justify the radical absence of a horizontal recognition, that of Luke is, on the contrary,
entirely led by a process of a horizontal recognition by the narrative's characters. How to explain this new orientation? The principal characteristic of the Lucan Passion narrative is indeed the progressive and paradoxical recognition of Jesus' innocence at the very

moment when the latter is jeered at and rejected. One will perhaps object that this motif is also encountered in Matthew/Mark, since right after the death of Jesus the centurion exclaims: "Truly this man was a son of God/innocent". Actually, in Luke, the recognition is described more systematically and extends to all the characters – except the Jewish religious authorities –, from the trial up to Jesus' death. And of what is it a recognition? Of Jesus' innocence. It is easy to note throughout the scenes the accumulated reactions and to show that the characters, more and more numerous, are aware of this innocence and show it more or less explicitly and directly, by their words and gestures:

Characters	Type of Recognition	Verses
Pilate	explicit and repeated	"I did not find this man guilty" 23:14 and 23:22
Herod	indirect	"neither did Herod, for he sent him back to us" 23:15
the women of Jerusalem	explicit and direct	"women who bewailed and lamented him." 23:27
the thief	explicit and direct	"this man has done nothing wrong." 23:41
the centurion	explicit and direct	"Certainly this man was innocent!" 23:47
all, at Calvary	indirect	"all the multitudes …returned home beating their breasts" 23:48

That Jesus' innocence in the Lucan Passion narrative has as well prophetic resonances is more than probable, for the unjust death of the prophets was then a well-known *topos*. Of course, the Lucan Passion narrative is not organized with the help of motifs taken from biblical narratives relating to the death of a prophet, but this comes from there not being one on the subject – except a few extrabiblical narratives, like in *The Martyrdom of Isaiah* and *The Lives of the Prophets*. It is the innocence of the prophets and the injustice of their death that Luke retains, a motif repeated several times by Jeremiah, who says he is righteous (Jer 53:11), to be, nevertheless, the object of a plot (Jer 18:2-3), and clearly proclaims his innocence before his opponents (Jer 26/33:15):

The recognition of innocence in Lk 23 is not as pronounced as that of the crowds and the disciples in Lk 9, who, respectively, saw in Jesus a great prophet and the Messiah, but it undeniably exists and, paradoxically, it is with it that the section of the Passion, where rejection is dominant, concludes. If it was important that the ministry began with the search for Jesus' identity and went as far as his recognition, varied but real in Lk 7–9, it is just as important that the section of the Passion end with the recognition of his innocence by numerous characters of the narrative. An essential recognition, for it responds to the requirements of the biographies of the time, where the protagonist's final recognition *by his contemporaries* was necessary. In other words, if the Lucan narrator has not repeated the psalmic model of the persecuted innocent like Mark and Matthew, a model that excludes any sort of horizontal *anagnôrisis*, it is because in writing for Greek listeners and readers, he had to honor the requirement of the biographies of that time where the protagonist was illustrious in the eyes of his contemporaries. Of course, Luke neither was able to nor wanted to eliminate the death on the cross and the mocking remarks that accompanied it – for it sealed the prophetic identity of Jesus –, but it is the recognition of his innocence by the actors in the narrative that finally prevails. By its paradoxical character – innocent and yet dying with criminals – the Lucan Passion narrative thus gives a response to the Jewish questions – the impossible death of the Messiah – and at the same time satisfies the Greek demand for a horizontal recognition.

The Typology in Luke 24

After the resurrection, Jesus declares to the two disciples who are on the road to Emmaus, then to the Eleven, that one can understand his messianic role and his itinerary only by rereading the Scriptures:

And he said to them, "O foolish men, and slow of heart to believe all that the prophets have spoken! [26] Was it not necessary that the Christ should suffer these things and enter into his glory? [27] And beginning with Moses and all the prophets, he interpreted to them in all the scriptures the things concerning himself. (Lk 24:25-27)

Two points merit a brief commentary: (i) the "was it not necessary?" and (ii) had all the prophets announced that the Messiah had to suffer in order to enter into his glory?

The "It Was Necessary" of the Sufferings
Several times over the course of his peregrinations (Lk 9:22; 13:33; 17:25), at the end of the Last Supper (Lk 22:37), and after his resurrection (Lk 24:7, 26, 44), Jesus recalls that it *is/was necessary* for him to pass through sufferings. How to understand this necessity? It is not as a good school boy who fills his pages with what he has been told to write but as a man who offers his freedom (Lk 22:41-44), without which the "it is necessary" loses its pertinence. It is because he is and knows himself to be a *prophet* that he must live to the bitter end the fate of the prophets: an unjust death and yet a death by which he is paradoxically going to be recognized innocent. The "it is necessary" of the unjust death is thus for the recognition of the true prophetic identity of Jesus.

Had the Scriptures Announced that the Messiah Would Suffer?
If one believes Jesus' declaration to the Eleven, after his resurrection, "Thus it is written, that the Christ should suffer and on the third day rise from the dead" (Lk 24:46), the Scriptures had in fact announced that the Messiah would suffer before being resurrected. In Acts 3:18 after the healing of the cripple at the Beautiful Gate, Peter repeats the same thing to the people who surround him, even emphasizing the fact that this was announced by *all* the prophets: "But what God foretold by the mouth of all the prophets, that his Christ should suffer." Yet, there was no expectation of a suffering Messiah. And if this were so, it is undoubtedly because the Scriptures had not explicitly announced it. Where can the reader thus

find in the Scriptures, in particular in the prophetic books, that the Messiah had to suffer? For, if one follows Luke's narrative, it is as Son of Man and as *prophet*, and not as *Messiah*, that Jesus, before his Passion, says he has to suffer and die unjustly. How, therefore, are the affirmations of Jesus and Peter after the resurrection to be understood? For it is only after the resurrection that Jesus and Peter after him say that the Messiah, a glorious and eschatological figure, first had to suffer. The resurrection had clearly caused the disciples to understand that Jesus was, henceforth, the announced glorious Messiah. It confirmed and sealed the itinerary of a Jesus faithful and obedient in everything to God his Father. If his glorious seat at the right of God as Messiah did not resolve the enigma of his igno-minious death on the cross, it, nevertheless, showed that this death could not be contrary to the ways of God. That is why the first dis-ciples searched the Scriptures for possible announcements and pre-figurements of this death that seemed to them unworthy of the glo-rious Messiah who was, henceforth, Jesus. The Passion narratives and the Gospels in their entirety show that their reading of the Scrip-tures was not sterile. Certainly, the resulting typology is not in itself messianic: the Jesus described in the Passion narratives indeed has the traits of the persecuted just of the supplications (in Mat-thew/Mark), of the prophets unjustly put to death (in Luke) and of the Pascal Lamb (in John); but this typology allows understanding why Jesus, the glorious Messiah, had to pass through the death that was his and why one could then say that it had been necessary for him to suffer and die rejected before entering into his glory. The multiple typology of the Passion narratives and more broadly of the Gospels thus gave to the figure of the Messiah a dimension that the sole title of Davidic descendent could not. Thanks to it, it was, henceforth, possible to announce that Jesus fulfilled all the Scrip-tures.

It is thus possible to respond to the interpretation that Erich Auerbach made of what he called the typological *method*. Of course, there is no link of causality between the type and the anti-type, but the relationship between Jesus and the figures of the

Scriptures is not artificial, for it is in rereading the life of Jesus that the disciples perceived the resemblances between the miracles that he had performed and those of Moses, Elijah and Elisha, between the sufferings that he had undergone and those of the prophets, in particular Jeremiah, but also those of the persecuted just of the Psalms of supplication. From these resemblances – the *synkriseis* – they understood that, all the while being the Messiah, he authentically belonged to the prophetic line and, progressively, that he was the one in whom all the Scriptures were fulfilled.

The Episode of the Ascension: A Priestly Typology or A Typology of Elijah?
   A Typology of Elijah
   We will admit, without any discussion, that the end of the Lucan narrative (Lk 24:50-52) again makes Elijah the type of Jesus, 2 Kings 2 being the only narrative of an ascension offered by the Old Testament. Semantic parallels, moreover, exist that authorize this reading:

2 Kings 2	Lk 24:50-52
Elijah taken to heaven,	Jesus carried to heaven,
Elisha, the disciple, sees him leave	the disciples see him leave
and receives a double share of his spirit	and are blessed

   As Elisha in 2 Kings 2 receives Elijah's spirit, which gives him the ability and power to act as a prophet following the example of his master, the blessing in Lk 24:50 has the role of pointing out that Jesus guarantees his disciples' future. It assures them of his support and his assistance.
   But does the blessing not indicate as well that Jesus is, henceforth, the High Priest, the all-powerful intercessor between God his Father and these same disciples? Of course, as we saw above regarding Lk 1:5-25, the Lucan narrator can in the same pericope allude to two, indeed several, texts from the Old Testament. Why then would Lk 24:50-52 not be referring to both 2 Kings 2 and Sir 50:20-21, Elijah and the High Priest both being types of Jesus?

A Priestly Typology[9]?

As we ascertained in ch. II, Lk 24:50-52 and Sir 50:20-21 have several words in common, and one has rightly read them synoptically, for they are the only passages from the New and Old Testament – Hebrew and Greek – where two rites of blessing have so many words in common[10]:

Sir 50:20-21	Lk 24:50-52
Then coming down he [the high priest Simon] *would raise his hands* over all the congregation of Israel. The *blessing* of the LORD would be upon his lips, the name of the LORD would be his glory. [21] they bowed down in *worship* a second time to receive the *blessing* of the Most High.	Then he [Jesus] led them [the disciples] out as far as Bethany, and *raising his hands* he *blessed* them. [51] While he *blessed* them, he parted from them. [52] And having *worshiped him* they returned to Jerusalem with great joy, and were continually in the temple *blessing* God.

We have also pointed out that Lev 9:22-24, where one finds the same vocabulary and the same background – the blessing of the people by the high priest Aaron – seems to confirm the priestly denotation. It is, on the other hand, true that if Jesus has the position of High Priest in Lk 24:50-52, the highlighted scriptural echo would be in a thematic coherence with the whole of the Lucan macro-narrative[11]: Jesus would have entered into heaven by becoming the High Priest, the one by whom our prayers, henceforth, definitively

---

[9] On the subject, let us recall the doctoral thesis of MEKKATTUKUNNEL, *The Priestly Blessing of the Risen Christ*, according to which the typology in Lk 24:50-52 is priestly.

[10] The words in common in the two passage are in italics. The table is reproducing the one from ch. II in order to facilitate the reading.

[11] One of Hays' criteria for there to be an allusion.

find favor from God. But, has we have already pointed out in ch. II, the vocabulary does not suffice. The semantic parallels are much more important. Is it certain that the High Priest – the Simon of Sir 50 or another, it does not matter – for it is only the function, and not the person, that can determine the reason for the parallel, if it exists – is the type of Jesus and that the faithful who were present at the worship, in Sir 50, are those of the disciples of Lk 24:50-52?

As Gen 48:8-20 shows, the vocabulary of blessing was not used only by priests. Additionally, two major difficulties exist that prohibit a true parallelism between the High Priest and Jesus! The first is that in Sir 50, the faithful prostrate themselves before God and not before the High Priest, whereas in Lk 24 it is Jesus who is the object of worship, as God. The reader will have perhaps noted, the verb used – in Greek, *proskynein* – has Jesus as its complement only at the end of the macro-narrative because being resurrected, glorious, he is, henceforth, Lord (in Greek, *kyrios*) and shares God's omnipotence. Before Lk 24, the narrator never said that any of the narrative's characters prostrated themselves before Jesus, the latter having himself declared during his stay in the desert that one must worship (*proskynein*) God alone (Lk 4:8 citing Deut 6:13).

A second difficulty, which does not affect the characters but the context, also makes priestly typology improbable. It is, of course, said that after the Ascension of Jesus, the disciples return to Jerusalem and are constantly in the Temple praising God (Lk 24:53). But, when Jesus blesses them, neither they nor he are in the Temple, whereas the blessing of the High Priest always occurred in this holy place. The shift is important and implies a priestly inter-pretation of the blessing given on the Mount of Olives is excluded. Perhaps it would be good to recall here what was said on the Mount of Olives at the time of the presentation of the entrance into Jerusa-lem in Mt 21.

The Lucan narrator's use of typology, in the end, prohibits seeing in Jesus the antitype of the high priests of the Old Testament. As we have seen, his manner of proceeding is indeed repetitive; the allusions to the characters from the biblical past presented as types of Jesus are found dispersed throughout the sections of his narrative;

Luke has the habit of several times returning to the same types, exclusively – or almost – prophetic. Yet, given this tendency for repetition, one would expect, if Jesus were in the position of High Priest in Lk 24:50-52, the Book of Acts to take up and repeat in its turn that Jesus is the High Priest, intercessor of our demands to God. Yet, there is nothing.

If the typological reading of Lk 24:50-52 cannot be priestly but is that of Elijah, why does the narrator describe Jesus in the process of blessing the disciples with apparently priestly gestures? Priests and high priests are not the only ones to bless. The Scriptures and the intertestamental writings mention blessings pronounced by the patriarchs and kings[12]. But over time and when after the return from the Exile the priestly body and the sacrificial cult became more and more important, the priestly blessing probably became the model of all blessing. The Lucan narrator – and perhaps already the writer of Sirach – thus seems to be repeating a *topos*.

VI. CONCLUSIONS

The manner in which the Lucan narrator and the Jesus of his narrative refer or allude to the Scriptures make it possible to formulate some conclusions:
- By taking up the words, the ideas and the figures from the Scriptures, the Lucan narrator wants to show that his narrative is in perfect continuity with them: it is *the same divine word* that announces the Good News, the promise of its realization. Unchanged is God,

---

[12] In addition to Gen 48:8-20, where one finds the same words (to bless, hand, to worship), see, for ex., the blessing pronounced by Solomon in 1 Kings 8:14 (= 2 Chron 6:3). Even if the gestures are not attributed to the same characters, one also finds in Neh 8:6 words in common with Sir 50:20-21 and Lk 24:50-52 that are indicative of the same cultural background: "And Ezra blessed the LORD, the great God; and all the people answered, "Amen, Amen," *lifting up their hands*; and they bowed their heads and *worshiped* the LORD with their faces to the ground." Also see *Joseph et Aseneth* 17:5-6.

the true one, the figures by which He reveals Himself being identical. Typology was for this reason essential to the Lucan narrative.

- For the Jesus of Luke in no way deviates from the promise and the ways by which God wanted it to be realized. Thanks to the prophetic typology, the Lucan narrative, in its way, seals the unity and the coherence of the ways of God.

- The function of the typological *synkrisis* is twofold: Jesus is recognizable as a prophet thanks to his words and his works but also and especially because his fate was similar, having been, like the prophets, persecuted, rejected and put to death by his coreligionists.

- The typological reading of Luke is above all attempting to show that Jesus belongs to the prophetic line, by his actions and by his violent death, and much less to imply that Jesus is superior to the prophets who have preceded him. In other words, the Lucan typology is above all based on the *synkriseis* and practically not on the preparation/fulfilment relationship, even less on the shadow/reality couplet.

- If, like Matthew, Luke develops an easily noted prophetic typology, they follow two different models for the Passion. Matthew follows the Marcan model of the supplications of the persecuted innocent in order to bring to its end the rejection and thus the absence of a final *anagnôrisis* on the part of the Israelites, whereas the Lucan Passion narrative is, on the contrary, entirely led by the process of a horizontal recognition on the part of the narrative's characters. Writing for Greeks, Luke had to highlight this horizontal recognition that was a part of the requirements for the biographies of that time.

- It is thanks to the prophetic typology that the messianic figure presented and achieved by Jesus becomes audible and receivable (*dektos*), that one may thus believe that "the Messiah [because also a prophet] had to suffer in order to enter into his glory".

CHAPTER VI

THE TYPOLOGY OF THE SYNOPTICS
SOME THESES

Perhaps it would be useful to recall, at the end of the journey, that typology is not the only method utilized by the three synoptic Gospels for constructing their protagonist Jesus. But even if, by its discretion, it remains unknown to many readers, typology is, nevertheless, the instrument without which the narrators' Christology would have suffered in its power and its range. But, will one say, was not Jesus' death confessed as salvific right after the resurrection, and did not the first disciples read Isaiah 53 in this way, well before the Synoptics appealed to the psalmic and prophetic typology? If it was faith that first enabled saying that the Messiah had to suffer in order to enter into his glory, it was, nevertheless, necessary to show that Jesus truly belonged, by his behavior and by his death, to the line of the prophets.

So that Jesus might be recognized as Messiah, suffering and rejected, Mark, Matthew and Luke thus had to have recourse to typology: this was the thesis developed over the course of the preceding chapters. This means, let us repeat, that the typology of the Synoptics is subordinate to the *anagnôrisis* and that without its use, there would never have been the Gospel narratives.

That said, as almost all the studies on biblical typology, centered on the relationship between the Old Testament type and the New Testament antitype, see in the first an announcement, an anticipation, indeed a preparation for the second that, by its superiority, brings to fulfillment the first, it is important to consider more carefully the process of the typological reading carried out by the Synoptics in order to revisit this interpretation.

But first, let us briefly present the results of the journey undertaken.

I. A BRIEF REPRISE OF THE JOURNEY

The Typology of Mark

In order to respond to the scandal of a Messiah rejected and crucified, Mark chose to read the Passion by having recourse to the supplications of the persecuted innocent because in these prayers the only *anagnôrisis* that matters is vertical: being in the position of the persecuted innocents, his prefigurations, Jesus neither could nor had to be recognized by anyone other than God. During his ministry, Jesus had been identified by the crowds with Elijah or one of the prophets of old. But one could always say that he had seduced and deceived the ignorant crowds and that his death on the cross had finally shown his true identity, that of a blasphemer. It thus was the recourse to the characters who were the types of the individual supplications that allowed resolving the question of the *anagnôrisis* and opened the door to the biographical genre for the first Christian writers.

Mark could have used the prophetic model, as will be done after him by Matthew and Luke, to say that Jesus was both recognized and rejected, like most of the prophets. By developing the two principal motifs of the prophetic model, recognition and rejection, he would have been able to show that the violent death was not contrary to Jesus' being-prophet, that, far from being counterproductive, the rejection and the death served, quite to the contrary, his identification as prophet. Why did he not emphasize the fact that being a prophet, Jesus could only have been, like the prophets, rejected and put to death by his coreligionists? If he did not do this, it is in order not to follow those who identified Jesus with Elijah, this prophet being for Mark the type of John the Baptist only. And

as neither Elijah nor Elisha were put to death by the Israelites of
their time, it was necessary for him to find another model, that of
the supplications of the persecuted innocent, in order to narrate the
Passion and death of his protagonist.

The Typology of Matthew

Like Mark, Matthew followed the psalmic model for the narrative of the Passion. But if for Mark, the psalmic model allowed
doing without any horizontal *anagnôrisis* – that of the people, but
also that of the disciples –, for Matthew the same model actually
served rather to show that the Israelites could go no further in their
refusal of the ways of God.

As to prophetic typology, it allowed the Matthean narrator to
show that, far from being opposed to each other, the recognition –
the *anagnôrisis* – and the rejection had to go hand in hand in order
to confirm Jesus' being-prophet.

The Matthean typology is Mosaic as well. Thanks to it, it was
possible to describe Jesus as the antitype of Moses the legislator,
whose precepts he brings to perfection, but also to make the book in
which Jesus' instructions are recorded the disciple's charter.

Matthew begins and ends his narrative with royal typology; it
allowed him to show that, if Jesus was not recognized as king/Mes-
siah, it is because of the chronic disobedience of his people.

The Typology of Luke

Let us recall that the typological reading of Luke attempts
above all to show that Jesus belongs to the prophetic line, by his
actions and by his violent death, and much less to imply that Jesus
is superior to the prophets who preceded him. In other words, the
Lucan typology is above all based on the *synkriseis* and not in practice on the preparation/fulfillment relationship, even less on the
shadow/reality pairing.

Matthew and Luke follow two different models for the Passion. The first takes up the Markan model of the supplications of

the persecuted innocent in order to bring to its conclusion the rejection and thus the absence of the final *anagnôrisis* on the part of the Israelites, whereas the narrative of the second is, on the contrary, entirely led by a process of horizontal recognition on the part of the narrative's characters.

Lastly, it is thanks to the prophetic typology that the messianic figure, essentially glorious for the Jewish tradition, was able to become audible, acceptable, that it is henceforth possible to believe the statements of Jesus in Luke 24:26 and of Peter in Acts 3:13, namely that "the Messiah *had* to suffer in order to enter into his glory".

In short, before being an interpretation of the inferiority of the type and the superiority of the antitype, the typology of the synoptic narratives is a search for traits and thus for types capable of showing Jesus' prophetic identity.

II. THE PROGRESSION OF THE TYPOLOGICAL READING

Let us briefly recall the two difficulties, initially insurmountable, for whomever had the crazy intention of writing a biography – a *bios* – of Jesus. In order to become a protagonist of a biography, he had to be illustrious, in other words to be recognized by his contemporaries. Having been rejected and put to death on the cross as a rebel and a blasphemer, Jesus could not in the eyes of his coreligionists become a national hero; lacking all the qualities that made up heroes – military victories, philosophical and scientific writings, great political discourses and other things, the Greek language and culture – he could not, moreover, be recognized by non-Jews. It was thus necessary to show that, notwithstanding these handicaps, Jesus merited a biography. But how to show it? My preceding essay had the object of presenting the biblical models thanks to which Mark, followed by Matthew and Luke, overcame the challenge.

But to this challenge – the absence of a horizontal *anagnôrisis* from his contemporaries – was added a second, a corollary to the first. Indeed, if by his resurrection, Jesus had become for the disciples the glorious royal figure awaited by the Jewish traditions, the rejection of which he had been the subject and his ignominious death were contrary to expectations; the Scriptures, indeed, did not announce a suffering Messiah. Yet, if the resurrection and the glorification confirmed Jesus' being-Messiah, his death could not be that of a rebel, an imposter or a blasphemer: it could not be unfamiliar or contrary to the ways of God. That is why Mark, Matthew and Luke revisited the Scriptures in order to search for characters, persecuted and rejected but nevertheless innocent and faithful, capable of accounting for Jesus' tragic destiny.

The first model was that of the persecuted faithful of the Psalms of supplication[1]. The work of the Markan narrator consisted of, after having noted and identified them, assembling all the motifs common to the Passion of Jesus and to the supplications of the persecuted innocent. The primary role of the paralleling – in other words, of the *synkrisis* – was to provide a model capable of overcoming the challenge posed by the necessity of an *anagnôrisis*. In short, it is principally in the supplications of the persecuted innocent and in the narratives relating to the prophets – Elijah, Elisha, Jeremiah – that Mark, Matthew and Luke have found the traits in common with Jesus' behavior and violent death. His death was no longer atypical; it was located within the line of the faithful and the prophets, rejected because of their being friends of God and heralds of His wills. As has been shown, the narratives of the Passion of Mark, Matthew and Luke repeat the motifs of the supplication of the persecuted innocent, without adding that there was a 'plus'; when Jesus announces that his fate will be that of the prophets, the 'plus' is still absent. In short, the primary goal of the *synkrisis* was not to show that the sufferings of the Old Testament types prefigure those of Jesus and that the latter brought to their fulfillment the sad fate.

But if with the sufferings and death, the typological reading has a goal of showing that Jesus is in direct continuity with the persecuted faithful and the prophets without adding that he is their

---

[1] Cf. ch. II of *The Birth of the Gospels*.

superior, on the other hand, with his thaumaturgical behavior and teaching, the 'plus' is present, implicitly, as in the narrative of the multiplication of the loaves[2], about which a commentator was able to declare: "Jesus, for his part, fulfilled the miracles of Elisha, by infinitely surpassing them"[3]; but also explicitly, as when, to those who asked of him a sign, Jesus responds that the sign will be that of the prophet Jonah, and adds: "something *greater than* Jonah is here"[4], or when, in the Sermon on the Mount, he repeats: "But I say to you"[5], bringing to their acme the commandments of the Mosaic Law.

If actually the typological reading of the synoptic narratives initially consisted in looking for and establishing parallels, it was then developed by pointing out Jesus' superiority over the Old Testament types. Not that the parallels between the type and the antitype were forgotten: – they remained primary, and without them there would not have been a typological reading –, but highlighting the omnipotence of Jesus, in his behavior and his teaching, was also essential to the Christology of the Synoptics. It would thus be precipitate to say that, in the Synoptics, Jesus' superiority does not belong to the typological reading. It is a part of it, but it is secondary and practically occurs only in the episodes preceding the Passion.

Lastly, what about the idea according to which the type would take its meaning from its fulfillment in the antitype and would thus become its prophecy? By far the idea preferred, since the Fathers of the Church, by theologians. The vocabulary of fulfillment is several times used by Matthew, particularly in the citations that he takes from the prophets, and one can, in some, note a figurative reading, as, for example, Mt 4:14-16 shows. In it, the narrator recounts

---

[2] Mk 6:35-44 = Mt 14:13-21 = Lk 9:10-17.
[3] VAN CANGH, *La multiplication des pains*, p. 66.
[4] Mt 12:41 = Lk 11:32.
[5] Mt 5:22,28,32,34,39,44.

where Jesus begins his ministry and adds that in this way the oracle of Isaiah[6] is fulfilled:

The land of Zebulun and the land of Naphtali, toward the sea, across the Jordan, Galilee of the Gentiles ... the people who sat in darkness have seen a great light, and for those who sat in the region and shadow of death light has dawned.

The text from Isaiah cited by Matthew is not only an oracle announcing the future salvation, for the luminous event was contemporaneous to the oracle: the prophecy refers to an event that occurred during his era. Matthew's reading is thus figurative, since it parallels two events separated in time, one from the past[7] and one from the present time of the coming of Jesus. Undoubtedly, the passage was chosen for the parallels between the characters (two kings, Hezekiah and the king-Messiah Jesus), the locales (Galilee and the surrounding regions) and the circumstances (the same people in misery). With the coming of Jesus, Galilee could not have received a greater light, one will willingly admit. But if Hezekiah is the prefiguration of Jesus, does the Matthean narrator make him as well a preparation, a prophecy of the messianic light? The very fact that he refers to the prophet Isaiah and says that his words find in Jesus their fulfillment[8] clearly indicates that, for him, the first event, the birth of the infant king at the time of Isaiah, was a prophecy of the luminous coming of Jesus. If one cannot find this (third) typological dimension in Mark or Luke, it is necessary to admit that it is present in Matthew, where the former events are prophecies of those that occurred with Jesus. We may note that the Matthean narrator was able, with strong analogies between the events from the biblical past and those from the time of Jesus, to say that the first prepared and

---

[6] Loosely cited from Isaiah 8:23-9:1.

[7] According to a number of commentators, it is a matter of the birth of King Hezekiah.

[8] On the sixteen occurrences of the Greek verb *plèroô* in Matthew, eight are in the third person singular passive aorist subjunctive, as in Mt 4:14 "that what was spoken by the prophet Isaiah might be fulfilled (*plèrôthè*)..."

announced the second without our being able to account for it exegetically. There begins the work of the theologian.

PART TWO

THE PROPHETIC TYPOLOGY
AND LUKE'S CULTURE

This second part does not treat the oxymoron presented in the first, but it seemed to me interesting to add a text that locates typology in relation to the manner in which the writings of the era, biographies but also novels, cited or alluded to great authors, in particular Homer. For if the utilization of typology in the gospel narratives came from the necessity of showing that Jesus was truly a prophet, by his deeds and by his death, the manner in which the gospel writers referred to Old Testament figures has numerous traits in common with the literary techniques of the writers of that day. There would have been no typology if the gospel writers had not in some way shared the culture of the writers of their time and had not known their literary techniques. This is particularly true for the author of the third Gospel, known as Luke. The lines that follow try to show that he had an above average culture and that his use of prophetic typology reveals his genius

CHAPTER VII

THE CULTURE OF THE NARRATOR OF LUKE/ACTS
FROM TECHNIQUES TO THEOLOGY

In recent decades, the question of the degree of the culture and literary quality of the author of the IIIrd Gospel and the Book of Acts has been discussed at length. The opinions of specialists are not uniform; for some, Luke read the Greek classics and clearly learned the techniques and subtleties of narrative writing, whereas for others, he remains a very average, if not to say mediocre, writer.

Various types of criteria are used: language (vocabulary, morphology, syntax), style (popular or not, because of the absence or presence of periods), intertextuality (citations and allusions to ancient classical authors), techniques (rhetoric, the ability to use and master the genres that at that time determined an author's fame). All specialists know these criteria; it is thus less their misunderstanding than their way of classifying them that influence their different judgements.

Is the author of Luke/Acts educated, and if the response is positive, how does he show it? Perhaps it would be good to present the respective positions and to propose our own interpretation of the information provided by Luke/Acts.

I. THE LANGUAGE OF LUKE/ACTS

Those who see in Luke a good historian and a good biographer do not primarily rely upon his language, for one does not find in

Luke/Acts the long periods of some writers of that time (especially Eastern) nor a pronounced Atticism – in other words, an imitation of the syntax and style of classical authors. By comparing the vocabulary in Luke with that of the classical language catalogued in the lexicon of Phrynichus[183], one can note about twenty words whose usage would not be correct[184]. As for the rules of syntax,

> [they] are reduced to a very few: no clauses that are called upon, that are complementary, that intertwine in order to form periods according to the harmonious hierarchy of Attic thought; the quite nuanced range of the tenses and modes of the Greek verb, will make a poor contribution… The statements are rather short, and more often, independent of each other… However, here and there, a trait breaks through that betrays in our author a knowledge of Greek syntax. Sometimes a strange resemblance to a classic text, however vague it may be, is there in order to certify that at least one of the great masters of Greek letters was not unknown to Luke … He wanted to be simple and achieved this, with his Hellenism at times showing itself[185].

If the phraseology of Luke/Acts is not the purest, let us not, however, forget that it is not primarily from ignorance but, for most cases, from a subtle imitation of the phraseology of the Greek Old Testament. Three examples, well-known by specialists, will suffice to show this:

- the expression [*kai*] *egeneto* [*de*] *en tô* + infinitive, that one encounters 20x in Luke (1x in Acts) and 45x in the Greek Bible[186],

---

[183] PHRYNICHUS ARABIUS, also called Phrynichus the Atticist, a Greek grammarian and lexicographer who lived in the IInd century and went to school in Bithynia under Marcus Aurelius and Commodus.
[184] As S. ANTONIADIS has done, *L'Évangile de Luc*, 113-116. The author herself recognizes that there are few.
[185] ID., 121-122.
[186] The most numerous occurrences are found in 2 Chron (6x), 2 Sam (5x), 1 Sam, 1 Kings and Ezra (4x). Elsewhere in the NT only in Mk 4:4.

- the *to prosôpon estêrisen* in Lk 9:51, that repeats the phrase *stêrizo ... to prosôpon* from the Books of Jeremiah and Ezekiel[187],
- the periphrastic imperfect (*eimi* in the imperfect followed by the present participle)[188], imitating the translation that the LXX makes of the Hebrew phrase *hyh* in the *qatal* or in the *wayyiqtol* + particple[189]

With some variations, the author of Luke/Acts even goes as far as repeating some phrases from the Greek Old Testament[190]. These examples of imitation also explain, in their way, the existence of expressions and statements quite distant from the classical Greek. And if it is true that Luke/Acts does not contain periods, this does not mean that their author totally ignores them. Thus, the two parts of the canticle of Zechariah (Lk 1:68-75 and 76-79) are each formed from a single period, whose chiastic composition justifies their syntactical arrangement often considered as obscure. One thus cannot say that the author of Luke/Acts ignored syntactical periods: if he uses them with such parsimony, it is because he has clearly opted for simplification.

In addition to the desire for simplification, the phenomenon of imitation, so important during the era, allows taking into account most of the particularities of the vocabulary and syntax of Luke/Acts.

---

[187] Cf. Jer 3:12; 21:10; Ezra 6:2; 13:17; 14:8; 15:7; 21:2; 21:7; 25:2; 28:21: 29:2; 38:2.

[188] 25x in Luke, 17x in Acts. The Greek Bible: 14x in 1 Mac; 13x in Gen; 12x in 2 Sam and 1 Kings; 10x in 1 Sam and Neh. In the NT, 10x in Mark.

[189] Cf. A. VERBOONEN, *L'imparfait périphrastique dans l'Évangile de Luc et dans la Septante*. Contribution à l'étude du système verbal néotestamentaire (Leuven 1992).

[190] Many of the verses of the canticles of Mary and Zechariah repeat expressions from the LXX: similarly, Luke 2:40 and 52 refer to 1 Sam 2:26; etc.

II. THE LITERARY MODELS OF LUKE/ACTS

The Biblical and Jewish Literary Models

For a long time, it has been accepted that the author of the IIIrd Gospel uses biblical models (hymns, genealogies, narratives of announcements of births by divine messengers, etc.) as well as Jewish models (controversies, parables, etc.). He, moreover, knows others, like the farewell discourse of Paul to the Elders of Ephesus (Acts 20:18-35), which clearly belongs to the testamentary genre[191], and of which one has tried, but wrongly, to show that it was imitating Hector's farewell to Andromache in Book VI of the Iliad (verses 440-455)[192]. In short, the familiarity of the narrator of Luke/Acts with biblical but also Jewish intertestamental writings and the literary modes that are found in them is undeniable.

The Two Prologues – Luke 1:1-4 and Acts 1:1-5

For thirty years, the two prologues, particularly Lk 1:1-4, have held the attention of exegetes. The most well-known study is that of L. Alexander[193], for whom it is not a preface[194] of the historical type, for the closest parallels belong to the Greek scientific tradition. Lk 1:1-4 would indeed be distinguished from historical prefaces in several regards: (1) the text is noticeably shorter and does not clearly state the contents of the book (name of the protagonist, etc.); (2) it is as well anonymous, whereas Greek historians state their name; (3) it contains a dedication that is missing in those prefaces, (4) which, moreover, do not use the first person singular ("I").

---

[191] A genre that was widespread in Judaism before and at the beginning of the Christian era.

[192] D. R. MacDonald, "Farewell to the Ephesian Elders", 189-203, who notes the numerous common motifs present in the Iliad, Book VI, and Acts 20:18-35 but misunderstands the model taken up by the author of Acts.

[193] L. Alexander, *The Preface to Luke's Gospel*.

[194] In Greek, *prooimion*, translated by preface or prologue.

It has been objected regarding Alexander's conclusions that Luke is not a scientific treatise – on geography, medicine, botany, etc. – and that, for this reason, Luke 1:1-4 could not be a preface of the same type[195]. Instead of the anonymity being due to the subject treated, it comes rather from the biographies of Jesus that had already been written and diffused – at least Mark, probably Matthew –, were themselves anonymous – Luke thus having to do as his predecessors. In the discussion on the scientific/historical alternative, the biographical genre seems to have been wrongly forgotten by Alexander, for the preface of Luke resembles, at least in length but with an added dedication, that of the *Vita Mosis* of Philo (1:1-4).

As just said, according to Alexander, Lk 1:1-4 cannot be a historical preface, for it does not name Jesus, the protagonist of the macro-narrative. To outline a pertinent response to this objection, it is necessary to take into account the clues from the narrator in the first chapters of the Gospel (Lk 1–2). Indeed, the first episodes do not first nor only speak of Jesus, but of the events related to the birth of John the Baptist; what is more, as narrator, Luke only calls Jesus by his name after the circumcision (2:21), thus obeying, with Mary, the angelic order (cf. 1:31); why would he have mentioned it before this episode, was it in a preface? But if this rhetorical vagueness was in part due to the scrupulous respect for the words of the angel and the uses reported by the narrative, it means as well that the narrator thus is enlisting discretion.

The Narrative Compositions

Specialists are divided on the narrative abilities of Luke. According to some, a comparison with classical biographers or historians would show that he is not a great narrator, and it does not seem very probable to them that he reached the highest level of studies[196].

---

[195] Cf. D. A. AUNE, "Luke: 1:1-4: Historical or Scientific *Prooimion*?", in ID., *Jesus, Gospel Tradition and Paul*, 107-115.
[196] Thus, O. PADILLA, "Hellenistic paideia and Luke's Education".

This opinion is far from being satisfactory. It is still necessary to take into consideration Luke's dual ability for imitation: many studies have emphasized his anthological style in the gospel narrative, where he discretely but extensively takes up entire passages from the Greek Bible[197], and in Acts, where the tenor of the discourses addressed to pagans is typically Greek, by the composition and the *topoi* used[198]. But it has above all been shown that, like Greek authors, Luke is capable of *ekphrasis*, of a detailed, technical and lively description. With the storm narrative in Acts 27:1–28:16 the scientific writing in Luke is as good as the descriptions of storms that preceded his[199]. I myself have shown how, in the narrative that is made of the Passion and death of Jesus, the Lucan narrator shows with finesse and genius how his protagonist is progressively recognized as innocent by the majority of the drama's actors, in spite of the false accusations and lies[200]. The hero of his biography thus receives the necessary recognition[201] of which he had to be the object.

---

[197] Cf. the articles of T. L. BRODIE, "Greco-Roman Imitation"; "Towards Unravelling Luke's Use of the Old Testament"; "Luke 7:36-50 as an Internalization of 2 Kings 4:1-37".

[198] Cf., for example, the essay of M. FATTAL, *Saint Paul face aux philosophes épicuriens et stoïciens* (Ouverture philosophique; Paris 2010) on Paul's discourse in Athens in Acts 17:22-31, showing that Luke (or the Paul of his narrative) knew the principle ideas of the philosophical schools of his time well; also the study of F. LESTANG, "A la louange du dieu inconnu. Analyse rhetorique de Ac 17,22-31", *NTS* 52 (2006) 394-408.

[199] C. REYNIER, *Paul de Tarse en Méditerranée*. Recherches autour de la navigation dans l'Antiquité (Ac 27,1-28,16) (LD 206; Paris 2006).

[200] J.N. ALETTI, *L'art de raconter Jésus Christ*. L'écriture narrative de l'évangile de Luc (Paris 1989) 155-177; ID., *Le Jésus de Luc* (Jésus et Jésus-Christ 98; Paris 2010) 157-184.

[201] In Greek, *anagnôrisis*.

The Synkrisis

A meticulous narrative approach to the Lucan diptych cannot but come to the conclusion that the author is a great narrator, very well aware of ancient Greek rhetoric as well as the biblical models of composition. Whether or not he undertook the *progymnasmata* can in the end only be determined if one takes into consideration his mastery of literary techniques, for, he has the art of composing, of developing a narrative, of reporting points of view, and especially of using the comparison[202], a technique that is well-known thanks to the writings of Plutarch and one that is spread throughout the whole of the Luke/Acts diptych.

For decades, exegetes have indeed noted in Acts the parallels that exist between Peter and Paul, parallels made in order to show that the testimony of Paul is as valid as Peter's[203].

But this *synkrisis* between the apostles is not the only one: there exists another, more fundamental, between Peter/Paul and Jesus that has the function of showing that the apostles ideally conform to what their master said and did[204]. Indirectly, the narrator of Luke/Acts thus responds to the accusations made against the first Christian generations: far from having perverted the Good News, those who had known Jesus before his death/resurrection, but also those who followed after them, represented by Paul, had announced and transmitted it impeccably.

By tracing the way in which the narrator of Luke/Acts uses the *synkrisis*, with finesse and discretion, one may rightly say that his mastery is by far superior to that which the *progymnasmata* would have been able to give him.

Greek Rhetoric

If the author of Luke/Acts is not only a capable narrator, he is as well a master of the genres and rules of Greek rhetoric, as one

---

[202] In Greek, *synkrisis*.
[203] J.-N. ALETTI, *Quand Luc raconte* (Paris 1998), 75-76.
[204] See the tables of the parallels in ALETTI, *Quand Luc raconte*, 80-96.

can see in the two discourses in Acts 17:22-31 and 24:16-21, the first being of the epidictic[205] type, and the second, judicial – because it is a defense[206]. In the Third Gospel, especially during the ascent to Jerusalem, which is a section more discursive than narrative, we also note the use of reasoning in the form of *chreiai,* which unfortunately few exegetes have identified (Lk 11:14-26; 12:13-21; 12:22-34).

More generally, the careful reader ascertains that the Lucan rhetoric changes with the addressees: the arguments are principally biblical when its addressees are Jewish, and Greek, when their audience is Greek. This ability to provide proofs chosen according to the audience, more than a vast culture, denotes a fine and creative intelligence. So what then is the culture, in other words, the knowledge that the author of the Luke/Acts diptych has of the great ancient and contemporary authors?

III. THE CULTURE OF THE AUTHOR OF LUKE/ACTS

The Biblical Citations and Allusions

In classical works, the culture of an orator or a writer was almost always denoted by the number of citations and allusions. That the third Gospel and the first part of Acts is stuffed with biblical reminiscences, today all accept; there is thus no longer need to prove it. But one may be surprised, with the commentators, by the absence

---

[205] Numerous exegetes have analyzed this discourse. Here I will only refer to LESTANG, "A la louange du dieu inconnu", 394-408, who has highlighted the progression of the argumentation and the different *topoi* used.
[206] It is Paul's defense speech before Felix in Acts 24: after a *captatio benevolentiae* (v. 10), the apostle responds to a first grievance by affirming that he has always remained faithful to the Law and to the Prophets (vv. 11-16), then to a second, by recounting what happened in the Temple and before the Sanhedrin (vv. 17-21).

of citations and allusions after Acts 15. The thought of J. Fitzmyer is, on this point, typical[207]:

> What is surprising is that the vast majority of the OT quotations appear in the first part of Acts, in chaps. 1–15. Only two (Ex 22:27 in Acts 23:5; and Isa 6:9-10 in 28:26-27) are found in the second part, where the story of Paul's missionary endeavors is recounted. The extent to which this may be due to sources that Luke has used can be debated. Most of the quotations in the first part occur also in speeches, especially those addressed to Jewish audiences, who would be expected to comprehend the quotations or allusions to the OT. There are also several global references in Acts to what God has "announced long ago through all the prophets" (3:18), or to what "all the prophets ... from Samuel on down ... have proclaimed" (3:24), or "to him [Jesus of Nazareth] all the prophets bear witness" (10:43). Such global references to the OT can be found further in 17:3; 18:28; 24:14; 26:22[208]. They are called "global" references, because they usually do not cite or allude to specific OT passages but summarize what God did or said in the OT and often use the Lucan hyperbolic "all". Moreover, such global references are almost exclusively Lucan in the NT and reveal a distinctively Lucan way of using the Scriptures of old.

Actually, if the apostle Paul's citations of and allusions to biblical passages practically disappear beginning with Acts 16, it is because the only discourse that he speaks, in Athens, is addressed to Greek philosophers and alludes to *topoi* that are familiar to them. In addition to the numerous allusions already noted by the commentators on this discourse, let us note that of v. 28: in this God that you do not know, says Paul, "we live" (*en autô zômen*). Yet, for the Greeks of that time the author of life was Zeus. Thus, Paul's listeners could not but think of the then known etymological connection between the god Zeus and the verb *zên* (to live).

If, for the reasons just pointed out, there are few biblical citations and allusions in the last chapters of Acts, the rest of the work, in particular the first section of the diptych, testifies to Luke's

---

[207] J.A. FITZMYER, *The Acts of the Apostles*. A New Translation with Introduction and Commentary (New Haven – London 2008) 91, §§ 76-77.
[208] Paul makes these generic references to the Scriptures before the Jews in order to protest his fidelity.

familiarity with the Scriptures in their entirety and not only the historical books (from 1 Sam to 2 Kings). The biblical material permeates the Lucan writing to such a degree that it structures the ministry of Jesus, thanks to the prophetic typology that takes into account the progression and choice of episodes in the IIIrd Gospel.[209]

The Allusions to the Great Greek Authors

As, in some passages, Luke explicitly cites Greek authors or alludes to them, one has deduced that he had to have had a quite extensive culture and had for this reason more or less taken up the *progymnasmata*, exercises referred to as preliminary, which today more or less correspond to secondary schools[210].

These are the passages most frequently mentioned for confirming this impression:

- Acts 5:39, where the Greek adjective *theomachoi*[211] used by Gamaliel could have come from the *Bacchae* of Euripides[212],

---

[209] In the first part of this essay, I have shown the decisive importance of prophetic typology. See ALETTI., "La typologie dans le troisième évangile. Son extension et son originalité", *Extra ironiam nulla salus*. Studi in onore di Roberto Vignolo in occasione del suo LXX compleanno (ed. M. CRIMELLA – G. C. PAGAZZI – S. ROMANELLLO) (Biblica 8, Milan 2016) 333-353.

[210] See, in the bibliography, the studies of M. C. PARSONS, "Luke and the *Progymnasmata*". 43-64; R. I. PERVO, *Profit with Delight*; M. MARTIN, "Progymnastic Topic Lists".

[211] "Who fight against (a) God" or "who oppose God/the gods".

[212] In verse 45 (Dionysius complains that Pentheus, the king of Thebes, by forbidding his cult *is making war against the divinity*, excludes libations, and, in his prayers, never mentions him) and 325 (Tiresias declares to the king Pentheus that his discourses will not succeed in convincing him to *fight the gods*). Euripides was, it seems, during that era, one of the authors favored for the formation of students. Cf. R. CRIBIORE, "'The Grammarians' Choice. The Popularity of Euripides' *Pheonissae* in Hellenistic and Roman Education", *Education in Greek and Roman Antiquity* (ed. Y. L. TOO) (Leiden 2001) 241-259.

- Acts 14:8-20, the episode at Lystra, where he alludes to the story of Zeus and Hermes being received by Philemon and Baucis[213],
- Acts 17:18, which alludes to the reproaches made against Socrates for preaching foreign doctrines and introducing a new religion[214],
- Acts 17:28, with a hypothetical allusion to Epimenides[215],
- Acts 17:28, a citation from Aratus[216],
- Acts 17:31, with a probable allusion to the *Eumenides* of Aeschylus[217],
- Acts 17, more globally, the context of the discourse at the Areopagus, with the background from the *Eumenides* of Aeschylus[218],

---

[213] A legend known today thanks to Ovid, *Metamorphosis*, 8:626-724. On the episode at Lystra, see D. P. BECHARD, *Paul Outside the Walls*. A Study of Luke's Socio-geographical Universalism in Acts 14:8-20 (AnBib 143; Rome 2000).

[214] XENOPHON, *Memorabilia* 1.1,1 "I have often asked myself by what arguments Socrates' accusers [291] persuaded the Athenians that he merited death like a criminal for the City. The accusation brought against him was thus approximately conceived: "Socrates is guilty of not recognizing the gods recognized by the City and of introducing new divinities (*etera kaina daimonia eispherôn*); he is also guilty of corrupting young men"".

[215] "It is in him that we have life, movement and being". Some, such as C. K. ROTHSCHILD, *Paul in Athens*. The Popular Religious Context of Acts 17 (WUNT 341; Tübingen 2014), see here an allusion to Epimenides the Cretan. But for many exegetes, this does not seem to be very probable.

[216] "We are of his race". ARATUS, *Phaenomena*, 5.

[217] ID., verse 647-648: "When the dust has drunk the blood of a dead man, he no longer can rise" (*andros d'epeidan haima anaspasè konis hapax thanontos outis est'anastasis*).

[218] As noted by, among others, LESTANG, "A la louange du dieu inconnu", 394-408, the choice of the place for Paul's discourse is intentional, for, according to what Aeschylus says in the *Eumenides*, the goddess Athena wanted to grant justice in a new way, thus allowing Orestes to escape the Eumenides. The Areopagus is the place among all others where Apollo put into crisis the traditional manner, represented by the Eumenides, of avenging blood, and with the help of Athena absolves Orestes, who was pursued and almost condemned to death... With Paul's discourse, the Areopagus becomes the place where the 'unknown god'

- Acts 20:35, where some see as well as a reminiscence of Thucydides[219],
- Acts 26:14[220], which repeats a Greek proverb, but that some
  see as well as being borrowed from the *Bacchae* of Euripides[221].
- One can as well be impressed, as S. Mason himself was, by
  some statements in Luke/Acts, incomprehensible if one does
  not accept that Luke probably knew and read Flavius Josephus[222].

The allusions to the *topoi* of Greek culture are numerous and
invite thinking that the author of Luke/Acts knew these *topoi* because he had at least gone through the *progymnasmata*. Some historians call for, it is true, prudence[223], for several of the verses from
Acts just mentioned could be referring to phrases that over time had
become proverbial rather than to a particular passage. As most of
the verses noted above are allusions, it is impossible to know if Luke
read the works of the authors or if he only collected several *topoi*
known at that time. But the discourse in Acts 17 allows responding
with more probability, for prudence would be appropriate in matters
of isolated phrases. Yet, far from only citing a sentence from

---

manifests his justice not towards a man who had committed the murder of his
mother but towards all men who put to death the one whom God raised from the
dead.

[219] *Historiae* 2.97.4. One finds in it the expression from Acts but in inverse order
(the rule of the Odrysians, says Thucydides, is "to receive rather than to give").
An idea proposed by E. PLÜMACHER, "Eine Thukydidesreminiszenz in der
Apostelgeschichte (Act 20,33-35 – Thuk. II 97.3f)", *ZNW* 83 (1992) 270-275.
[220] "To kick against the goads" (in Greek, *pros kentra laktizein*).
[221] Verse 794. Acts 26:14 and the *Bacchae* have the same expression *pros kentra
laktizein*.
[222] S. MASON, *Josephus and the New Testament* (Peabody, MA ²2003), all of ch.
6.
[223] See, among others, PADILLA, "Hellenistic paideia and Luke's Education", 416-
437, where one will find all the argumentation. One would also benefit from
consulting the article by J. J. KILGALLEN, "Acts 20:35 and Thucydides 2.97.4"
JBL 112 (1993) 480-506.

Aratus, this discourse makes multiple pertinent allusions to the ideas of the ancient philosophical schools and to knowledge that is in no way superficial. Why would what is valid for this discourse not be valid for the allusions disseminated throughout the remainder of the Book of Acts? The culture of the author of the Luke/Acts diptych is more extensive and solid than is generally thought.

IV. CULTURE AND THEOLOGY IN LUKE/ACTS

The preceding lines have wanted to show that one cannot judge the culture of Luke only by noting the citations and allusions that he makes. It is also necessary to take into account his narrative and rhetorical mastery. In short, it is not only by the intertextuality or the allusions/citations of earlier and contemporary Greek authors that one can determine the cultural level of Luke.

Let us go further. Luke's abundant repetition of biblical phraseology and models is not just to display his culture. It is the means by which he shows that the message of Jesus and of his disciples is rooted in the Scriptures and that there is complete continuity beween the holy books of Israel and what the characters in his diptych say and live. By affirming that Jesus and his disciples have neither distorted nor perverted the truth of the biblical books but that their message is its fulfillment, Luke indirectly responds to those who accused the Jesus-movement of having introduced a new religion.

By citing or making allusions to Greek authors, Luke wants to point out that the announcement of the Good News is not made by a negation of cultures. For him, the Good News can and must be announced in different cultures and dialogued with them. The Book of Acts is perhaps one of the first examples of inculturation of the Gospel.

BIBLIOGRAPHY

Adna J., « Der Gottesknecht als triumphierender und interzessorischer Messias. Die Rezeption von Jes 53 im Targum Jonathan untersucht mit besonderer Berücksichtigung des Messiasbildes », dans Janowski Bernd und Stuhlmacher Peter (ed), *Der leidende Gottesknecht*. Jesaja 53 und seine Wirkungsgeschichte, Mohr Siebeck, coll. Forschungen zum Alten Testament 14, Tübingen, 1996, p. 129-158.

Aletti J.N., *Quand Luc raconte* (LB), Paris 1998.

_____, « De l'usage des modèles en exégèse biblique. Le cas de la mort de Jésus dans le récit marcien », dans Vincente Collado Bertomeu (éd.), *Palabra, prodigio, poesìa*, FS Luis Alonso Schökel, Pontificio Istituto Biblico, coll. AnBib 151, Rome, 2003, p. 337-348.

_____, *Jésus, une vie à raconter*. Essai sur le genre des évangiles de Matthieu, Marc et Luc, Lessius, coll. Le livre et le rouleau, Namur, 2016.

Alexander L., *The Preface to Luke's Gospel*. Literary Convention and Social Context in Luke 1.1-4 and Acts 1.1-5 (SNTSMS 78; Cambridge 1993).

Allison D. C., *The New Moses*. A Matthean Typology, T&T Clark, Minneapolis, 1993.

Antoniadis S., *L'Évangile de Luc*, Esquisse de grammaire et de style (Collection de l'institut néo-hellénique 7), Paris 1930.

Aune D.A., "Luke: 1:1-4: Historical or Scientific *Prooimion*?", Id., *Jesus, Gospel Tradition and Paul in the Context of Jewish and Greco-Roman Antiquity* (WUNT 303; Tübingen 2013), 107-115.

Baker D.L., «Typology and the Christian Use of the Old Testament», in *ScotJournTheol* 29, 1976, p. 137-157.

Beauchamp P., « Le Pentateuque et la lecture typologique », in P. Haudebert (ed.), *Le Pentateuque. Débats et recherches*, Cerf (LD 151), Paris, 1992, p. 241-258.

_____, « Accomplir les Écritures. Un chemin de théologie biblique », in *RB* 99, 1992, p. 132-162.

_____, L'interprétation figurative et ses présupposés », in *RSR* 63, 1975, p. 299-312.

_____, « La figure dans l'un et l'autre Testament », in *RSR* 59, 1971, p. 209-224.

_____, « Lecture christique de l'Ancien Testament », dans *Bib* 81, 2000, p. 105-115.

Beaude P.M., « N'y a-t-il d'accomplissement que chrétien ? », in *RevSR* 68 (1994) 325-336.

Bechard D.P., *Paul Outside the Walls*. A Study of Luke's Sociogeographical Universalism in Acts 14:8-20 (AnBib 143; Rome 2000).

Benzi G., « L'esegesi figurale in Paul Beauchamp », in *Teologia* 42, 2002, p. 35-51.

_____, « Per una riproposizione dell'esegesi figurale secondo la prospettiva di P. Beauchamp », dans *RivBib* 42, 1994, p. 129-178.

Brodie T.L., « Luke 7,36-50 as an Internalization of 2 Kings 4,1-37: A Study in Luke's Use of Rhetorical Imitation », dans *Bib* 64, 1983, p. 457-485.

_____, "Greco-Roman Imitation of Texts as a Partial Guide to Luke's Use of Sources", *Luke-Acts* (ed. C. H. TALBERT) (New Perspectives from the Society of Biblical Literature; New York, NY 1984) 17-46.

_____, « Towards Unraveling Luke's Use of the Old Testament: Luke 7:11-17 as an *Imitatio* of 1 Kings 17: 17-24 », in *NTS* 32, 1986, p. 247-267.

Bultmann R., «Ursprung und Sinn der Typologie als hermeneutischer Methode», dans *ThLZ* 75, 1950, p. 205-212.

Cahill P.J., « Hermeneutical Implications of Typology », in *CBQ* 44, 1982, p. 266-281..

Carmignac J., « Pourquoi Jérémie est-il mentionné en Matthieu, 16,14 ? », in G. Jeremias (ed.), *Tradition und Glaube. Das frühe Christentum in seiner Umwelt* (FS K.G. Kuhn), Vandenhoeck & Ruprecht, Göttingen, 1971, p. 283-298.

Cribiore R., "'The Grammarians' Choice. The Popularity of Euripides' *Pheonissae* in Hellenistic and Roman Education", *Education in Greek and Roman Antiquity* (ed. Y.L. Too) (Leiden 2001) 241-259.

Damm A., « A Rethorical-Critical Assessment of Luke's Use of the Elijah-Elisha Narrative », dans John S. Kloppenborg – Joseph Verheyden (ed.), *The Elijah-Elisha Narrative in the Composition of Luke,* Bloomsbury, coll. LNTS 493, London, 2014, p. 88-112.

Dautzenberg G., « Elija im Markusevangelium », in Frans Van Segbroeck (éd.), *The Four Gospels* (FS F. Neirynck), Peeters, coll. BETL 100, Leuven 1992, vol.2, p. 1077-1094.

_____, *Studien zur Theologie der Jesustradition*, Katholisches Bibelwerk, coll. SBA 191, Stuttgart, 1995, p. 352-375.

Davidson R.M., *Typology in Scripture*: *A Study of Hermeneutical* τύπος *Structures*, Andrews University Press, Berrien Springs, MI, 1981.

Dawson J.D., *Christian Figural Reading and the Fashioning of Identity*, University of California Press, Berkeley, 2002.

Deneken M., « Jésus de Nazareth fondement atypique de la typologie chrétienne », in Raymond Kuntzmann (éd.), *Typologie biblique. De quelques figures vives*, Cerf, coll. LD hors-série, Paris, 2002, p. 241-266.

Donaldson T.L., *Jesus on the Mountain*. A Study in Matthean Theology, JSOT Press, coll. JSOT Sup Series 8, Sheffield, 1985.

Dubois J.D., « La figure d'Élie dans la perspective lucanienne », in *RHPR* 53, 1973, p. 155-176.

Eichrodt W., « Is Typological Exegesis an Appropriate Method ? », in C. Westermann (ed.), *Essays on Old Testament*

Hermeneutics, John Knox, Richmond, VA, 1963, p. 224-245. Original allemand : „Ist die typologische Exegese sachge-mäße Exegese?" dans *ThLZ*, 1956, p. 641-654.

Ellis E.E., « Biblical Interpretation in the New Testament Church », in M. J. Mulder (ed.), *MIKRA. Text, Translation, Reading and Interpretation of the Hebrew Bible in Ancient Judaism and Early Christianity*, Hendrickson Publisher, Peabody, MA, 2004, p. 691-725.

Fishbane M., *Biblical Interpretation in Ancient Israel*, Clarendon Press, Oxford, 1985.

Fitzmyer J.A., *The Acts of the Apostles*. A New Translation with Introduction and Commentary, New Haven – London 2008.

Foster P., « Echoes without Resonance: Critiquing Certain Aspects of Recent Scholarly Trends in the Study of Jewish Scriptures in the New Testament », in *JSNT* 38, 2015, p. 96-111.

France R.Th., *Jesus and the Old Testament. His Application of Old Testament Passages to Himself and his Mission*, The Tyndale Press, London, ²1994 (1971).

Frye N., *The Great Code. The Bible and Literature*, Harcourt Brace Jovanovich, New York, 1982.

Goppelt L., *Typos. The Typological Interpretation of the Old Testament in the New*, Eerdmans, Grand Rapids, 1982.

Goulder M.D., *Type and History in Acts*, S.P.C.K., London, 1964.

Grogan G.W., « The Relationship between Prophecy and Typology », in *Scottish Bulletin of Evangelical Theology* 4, 1986, p. 5-16.

Gundry R.H., *The Use of the Old Testament in St Matthew's Gospel*, Brill, Leiden, 1967.

Harris S., *The Davidic Shepherd King in the Lukan Narrative*, T&T Clark - Bloomsbury, coll. LNTS 558, London, 2016.

Hays R.B., *Echoes of Scripture in the Letters of Paul*, Yale University Press, New Haven, CT, 1989.

Hengel M., « Zur Wirkungsgeschichte von Jes 53 in vorchristlicher Zeit », in Janowski Bernd und Stuhlmacher Peter (ed), *Der leidende Gottesknecht*. Jesaja 53 und seine

Wirkungsgeschichte, Mohr Siebeck, coll. Forschungen zum Alten Testament 14, Tübingen, 1996, p. 49-91.

Horsley R.A., « "Like One of the Prophets of Old". Two Types of Popular Prophets at the Time of Jesus», in *CBQ* 47, 1985, p. 435-463.

Hugenberger G.P., «Introductory Notes on Typology», in *ScotJournTheol* 29, 1976, p. 331-341.

Huizenga L.A., *The New Isaac. Tradition and Intertextuality in the Gospel of Matthew*, Brill, coll. NovT Sup 131, Leiden, 2009.

Hummel H.D., «The Old Testament Basis of Typological Interpretation», in *Biblical Research* 9, 1964, p. 38-50.

Husser J.M., « La typologie comme procédé de composition dans les textes de l'Ancien Testament », in Kuntzmann, R. (ed.), *Typologie biblique:* De quelques figures vives, Cerf, coll. LD hors-série, Paris, 2002, p. 11-34.

Jackson B.S., « Jésus et Moïse. Le statut du prophète à l'égard de la loi », in *Revue historique de droit français et étranger* 59 (1981) 341-360. Orig. Engl.: « The Prophet and the Law in Early Judaism and the New Testament », *Cardozo Studies in Law and Literature* 4, 1992, p. 123-166.

Katz P., « Jesus als Vorläufer des Christus. Mögliche Hinweise in den Evangelien auf Elia als den 'Typos Jesu' », in *TZ* 52, 1996, p. 225-235.

Kilgallen J.J., "Acts 20:35 and Thucydides 2.97.4" *JBL* 112 (1993) 480-506.

Kimball Ch.A., *Jesus' Exposition of the Old Testament in Luke's Gospel*, Sheffield Academic Press, coll. JSNT 94, Sheffield,1994.

Knowles M., *Jeremiah in Matthew's Gospel. The Rejected-Prophet motif in Matthaean Redaction*, Sheffield Academic Press, coll. JSNT Sup 68, Sheffield, 1993.

Kuntzmann R. (éd.), *Typologie biblique. De quelques figures vives*, Cerf, coll. LD hors-série, Paris, 2002.

Lampe G.W.H. - Woollcombe, K.J., *Essays on Typology*, SCM, London, 1957.

Lestang F., « À la louange du dieu inconnu. Analyse rhétorique de Ac 17.22–31 », *NTS* 52 (2006) 394-408.

Lunn N.P., « Allusions to the Joseph Narrative in the Synoptic Gospels and Acts. Foundations of a Biblical Type», in *JETS* 55, 2012, p. 27-41.

MacDonald D.R., "Farewell to the Ephesian Elders and Hector's Farewell to Andromache. A Strategic Imitation of Homer's Iliad", *Contextualizing Acts*. Lukan Narrative and Greco-Roman Discourse (ed. T. Penner – C. van der Stichele) (SBL Symposium Series 20; Atlanta, GA 2003), 189-203.

Marcus J., *The Way of the Lord*. Christological Exegesis of the Old Testament in the Gospel of Mark, T & T Clark,, Edinburgh, 1993.

Martin M., "Progymnastic Topic Lists. A Compositional Template for Luke and Other *Bioï*", *NTS* 54 (2008) 18-41.

Mason S., *Josephus and the New Testament*, Peabody, MA ²2003.

Mekkattukunnel A.G., *The priestly blessing of the Risen Christ. An Exegetico-Theological Analysis of Luke 24,50-53*, Peter Lang (European university studies. Series XXIII;Theology 714), Lang, Frankfurt am Main, 2001.

Menken M.J.J., « The References to Jeremiah in the Gospel According to Matthew», in *ETL* 60, 1984, p. 5-24.

Miller R.J., « Elijah, John and Jesus in the Gospel of Luke », in *NTS* 34, 198, p. 611-622.

Minear P.S., *To Heal and to Reveal. The Prophetic Vocation According to Luke*, Crossroad Book - Seabury Press, New York, NY, 1976.

Moessner D.P., « Luke 9,1-50: Luke's Preview of the Journey of the Prophet like Moses of Deuteronomy », in *JBL* 102, 1983, p. 575-605.

Moo D.J., *The Old Testament in the Gospel Passion Narratives*, The Almond Press, Sheffield 1983.

Nieuviarts J., *L'entrée de Jésus à Jérusalem* (Mt 21,1-17). Messianisme et accomplissement des Écritures en Matthieu, Cerf, coll. LD 176, Paris, 1999.

Ostmeyer K.H., « Typologie und Typos. Analyse eines schwierigen Verhältnisses », in *NTS* 46, 2000, p. 112-131.

Padilla O., "Hellenistic paideia and Luke's Education. A Critique of Recent Approaches", *NTS* 55 (2009) 416-437.

Parsons M.C., "Luke and the *Progymnasmata*. A Preliminary Investigation into the Preliminary Exercises", *Contextualizing Acts* (ed. Penner – van der Stichele), 43-64.

Pellegrini S., *Elija - Wegbereiter des Gottessohnes.* Eine textsemiotische Untersuchung in Markusevangelium, Herder, Freiburg, 2000.

Pervo R.I., *Profit with Delight.* The Literary Genre of the Acts of the Apostles, Philadelphia, PA 1987.

Plümacher E., "Eine Thukydidesreminiszenz in der Apostelgeschichte (Act 20,33-35 – Thuk. II 97.3f)", *ZNW* 83 (1992) 270-275.

Poirier J.C., « Jesus as an Elijanic Figure in Luke 4:16-30 », in *CBQ* 71, 2000, p. 349-363.

Powery E.B., *Jesus Reads Scripture.* The Function of Jesus' Use of Scripture in the Synoptic Gospels, Brill, Leiden, 2003.

Rad G. von, « Typological Interpretation of the Old Testament », in *Interpretation* 15, 1961, p. 174-192.

Rindoš J., *He of Whom It Is Written. John the Baptist and Elijah in Luke*, Peter Lang, coll. OBS 38, Frankfurt am Main, 2010.

Römer Th., « Typologie exodique dans les récits patriarcaux », in R. Kunztmann (ed.), *Typologie biblique. De quelques figures vives*, Cerf, coll. LD hors-série, Paris, 2002, p. 49-76.

Rothschild C.K., *Paul in Athens.* The Popular Religious Context of Acts 17 (WUNT 341), Tübingen 2014.

Sonnet, J.P., « De la généalogie au "Faites disciples" (Mt 28,19). Le livre de la génération de Jésus », in C. Focant - A. Wénin (éd.), *Analyse narrative et Bible. Deuxième colloque international du RRENAB, Louvain-La-Neuve, avril 2004*, coll. Peeters, BETL 191, Leuven, 2005, p. 199-209.

Sparks K.L., « Gospel as Conquest: Mosaic Typology in Matthew 28:16-20 », in *CBQ* 68, 2006, p. 651-663.

Stek J.H., « Biblical Typology Yesterday and Today », in *Calvin Theological Journal* 5, 1970, p. 133-162.

Verboonen A., *L'imparfait périphrastique dans l'Évangile de Luc et dans la Septante*. Contribution à l'étude du système verbal néotestamentaire (Leuven 1992).

Verheyden J., « Calling Jesus Prophet, as Seen by Luke», in J. Verheyden – K. Zamfir – T. Nicklas (éd.), *Prophets and Prophecy in Jewish and Early Christian Literature*, Mohr Siebeck, coll. WUNT 286, Tübingen, 2010, p. 177-210.

Watts R.E., *Isaiah's New Exodus in Mark*, Mohr Siebeck, coll. WUNT 288, Tübingen 1997.

Winkle R.E., « The Jeremiah Model for Jesus in the Temple», dans *Andrews University Seminary Studies* 24, 1986, p. 155-172.

INDEX OF ANCIENT AUTHORS

INDEX OF MODERN AUTHORS

Finito di stampare
nel mese di aprile 2022
dalla
Scuola Tipografica S. Pio X
Via degli Etruschi, 7
00185 Roma